# Further and Higher Education Act 1992

## 1992 CHAPTER 13

An Act to make new provision about further and higher education.
[6th March 1992]

**B**E IT ENACTED by the Queen's most Excellent Majesty, by and with the advice and consent of the Lords Spiritual and Temporal, and Commons, in this present Parliament assembled, and by the authority of the same, as follows:—

## PART I

### FURTHER EDUCATION

### CHAPTER I

### RESPONSIBILITY FOR FURTHER EDUCATION

#### *The new funding councils*

1.—(1) There shall be established—

(a) a body corporate to be known as the Further Education Funding Council for England to exercise in relation to England the functions conferred on them, and

(b) a body corporate to be known as the Further Education Funding Council for Wales to exercise in relation to Wales the functions conferred on them.

(2) The Further Education Funding Council for England shall consist of not less than twelve nor more than fifteen members appointed by the Secretary of State, of whom one shall be so appointed as chairman.

(3) The Further Education Funding Council for Wales shall consist of not less than eight nor more than twelve members appointed by the Secretary of State, of whom one shall be so appointed as chairman.

The Further Education Funding Councils.

(4)  In appointing the members of a council the Secretary of State—

(a)  shall have regard to the desirability of including persons who appear to him to have experience of, and to have shown capacity in, the provision of education or to have held, and to have shown capacity in, any position carrying responsibility for the provision of education and, in appointing such persons, he shall have regard to the desirability of their being currently engaged in the provision of further education or in carrying responsibility for such provision, and

(b)  shall have regard to the desirability of including persons who appear to him to have experience of, and to have shown capacity in, industrial, commercial or financial matters or the practice of any profession.

(5)  In this Part of this Act any reference to a council is to a further education funding council.

(6)  References in the Education Acts to the appropriate further education funding council, in relation to any educational institution—

(a)  where the institution mainly serves the population of England, are to the Further Education Funding Council for England and, where the institution mainly serves the population of Wales, are to the Further Education Funding Council for Wales, and

(b)  where the institution receives financial support from a further education funding council, are to that council also (if different).

(7)  Any dispute as to whether any functions are exercisable by one of the councils shall be determined by the Secretary of State.

(8)  Schedule 1 to this Act has effect with respect to each of the councils.

### The new further education sector

Full-time
education for 16
to 18 year-olds.

**2.**—(1) It shall be the duty of each council to secure the provision for the population of their area of sufficient facilities for education to which this subsection applies, that is, full-time education suitable to the requirements of persons over compulsory school age who have not attained the age of nineteen years.

(2)  That duty extends to all persons among that population who may want such education and have not attained the age of nineteen years.

(3)  A council shall discharge that duty so as—

(a)  to secure that the facilities are provided at such places, are of such character and are so equipped as to be sufficient to meet the reasonable needs of all persons to whom the duty extends, and

(b)  to take account of the different abilities and aptitudes of such persons.

(4)  A council may secure the provision of facilities for education to which subsection (1) above applies for persons to whom that duty does not extend.

(5)  A council shall discharge their functions under this section so as to make the most effective use of the council's resources and, in particular, to avoid provision which might give rise to disproportionate expenditure.

(6) In discharging those functions a council shall have regard to any education to which subsection (1) above applies provided by schools maintained by local education authorities, grant-maintained schools, special schools not maintained by local education authorities, city technology colleges or city colleges for the technology of the arts.

**3.**—(1) It shall be the duty of each council to secure the provision for the population of their area of adequate facilities for education to which this subsection applies, that is—

Part-time education, and full-time education for those over 18.

> (a) part-time education suitable to the requirements of persons of any age over compulsory school age, and

> (b) full-time education suitable to the requirements of persons who have attained the age of nineteen years,

where the education is provided by means of a course of a description mentioned in Schedule 2 to this Act.

(2) A council shall discharge that duty so as—

> (a) to secure that facilities are provided at such places, are of such character and are so equipped as to meet the reasonable need for education to which subsection (1) above applies, and

> (b) to take account of the different abilities and aptitudes of persons among that population.

(3) A council may secure the provision of facilities for education to which subsection (1) above applies where they are not under a duty to do so.

(4) A council shall discharge their functions under this section so as to make the most effective use of their resources and, in particular, to avoid provision which might give rise to disproportionate expenditure.

(5) In discharging those functions a council shall have regard to any education to which subsection (1) above applies provided by institutions outside the further education sector or higher education sector.

(6) The Secretary of State may by order amend Schedule 2 to this Act.

**4.**—(1) In exercising their functions under sections 2 and 3 of this Act, each council shall (subject to the provisions of those sections) do so in accordance with subsections (2) to (4) below.

Persons with learning difficulties.

(2) Each council shall have regard to the requirements of persons having learning difficulties.

(3) A council shall, if they are satisfied in the case of any person among the population of their area who has a learning difficulty and is over compulsory school age but has not attained the age of twenty-five years, that—

> (a) the facilities available in institutions within the further education sector or the higher education sector are not adequate for him, and

> (b) it is in his best interests to do so,

secure provision for him at an institution outside those sectors.

(4) A council shall, if they are satisfied that they cannot secure such provision for a person as they are required to secure under subsection (3) above unless they also secure the provision of boarding accommodation for him, secure the provision of boarding accommodation for him.

(5) In exercising their functions under sections 2 and 3 of this Act in the case of any person who has a learning difficulty and is over compulsory school age, a council may—

(a) if they are satisfied that the facilities available in institutions within the further education sector or the higher education sector are not adequate for him, secure provision for him at an institution outside those sectors, and

(b) secure the provision of boarding accommodation for him.

(6) Subject to subsection (7) below, for the purposes of this section a person has a "learning difficulty" if—

(a) he has a significantly greater difficulty in learning than the majority of persons of his age, or

(b) he has a disability which either prevents or hinders him from making use of facilities of a kind generally provided by institutions within the further education sector for persons of his age.

(7) A person is not to be taken as having a learning difficulty solely because the language (or form of the language) in which he is, or will be, taught is different from a language (or form of a language) which has at any time been spoken in his home.

### *Finance*

Administration of
funds by councils.

**5.**—(1) A council may give financial support to the governing body of any institution within the further education sector or the higher education sector in respect of—

(a) the provision of facilities for further education, or

(b) the provision of facilities, and the carrying on of any activities, which the governing body of the institution consider necessary or desirable to be provided or carried on for the purpose of or in connection with the provision of facilities for further education.

(2) A council may give financial support to the governing body of any institution within the further education sector in respect of—

(a) the provision of facilities for higher education, or

(b) the provision of facilities, and the carrying on of any activities, which the governing body of the institution consider necessary or desirable to be provided or carried on for the purpose of or in connection with the provision of facilities for higher education.

(3) A council may give financial support to a further education corporation for the purposes of any educational institution to be conducted by the corporation, including the establishment of such an institution.

(4) For the purposes of section 4(3) to (5) of this Act, a council may give financial support to any person other than a local education authority, the governing body of a grant-maintained school or a person maintaining or carrying on a city technology college or city college for the technology of the arts.

(5) A council may give financial support to any person in respect of—

    (a) the provision of training or advice, or

    (b) the carrying on of research or other activities,

relevant to the provision of facilities for further education.

(6) Financial support under this section—

    (a) shall take the form of grants, loans or other payments, and

    (b) may be given on such terms and conditions as the council think fit.

(7) The terms and conditions on which a council make any grants, loans or other payments under this section may in particular—

    (a) enable the council to require the repayment, in whole or in part, of sums paid by the council if any of the terms and conditions subject to which the sums were paid is not complied with, and

    (b) require the payment of interest in respect of any period during which a sum due to the council in accordance with any of the terms and conditions remains unpaid,

but shall not relate to the application by the person to whom the financial support is given of any sums derived otherwise than from the council.

(8) A council may not give any financial support except in accordance with this section.

6.—(1) Before exercising their discretion under section 5(1) to (4) of this Act with respect to the terms and conditions to be imposed in relation to any grants, loans or other payments, a council shall consult such of the following bodies as appear to the council to be appropriate to consult in the circumstances—     *Administration of funds: supplementary.*

    (a) such bodies representing the interests of institutions within the further education sector as appear to the council to be concerned, and

    (b) the governing body of any particular institution within that sector which appears to the council to be concerned.

(2) In exercising their functions in relation to the provision of financial support under section 5 of this Act a council shall have regard to the desirability of not discouraging any institution in respect of which such support is given from maintaining or developing its funding from other sources.

(3) In exercising those functions a council shall have regard (so far as they think it appropriate to do so in the light of any other relevant considerations) to the desirability of maintaining what appears to them to be an appropriate balance in the support given by them as between institutions of a denominational character and other institutions.

(4) For the purposes of subsection (3) above an institution is an institution of a denominational character if it appears to the council that either—

(a) at least one quarter of the members of the governing body of the institution are persons appointed to represent the interests of a religion or religious denomination,

(b) any of the property held for the purposes of the institution is held upon trusts which provide that, in the event of the discontinuance of the institution, the property concerned shall be held for, or sold and the proceeds of sale applied for, the benefit of a religion or religious denomination, or

(c) any of the property held for the purposes of the institution is held upon trust for or in connection with—

(i) the provision of education, or

(ii) the conduct of an educational institution,

in accordance with the tenets of a religion or religious denomination.

(5) Where—

(a) the governing body of an institution within the further education sector to which this subsection applies ("the sponsoring body") receive from the governing body of an institution outside that sector ("the external institution") a request for the sponsoring body to apply to a council for financial support in respect of the provision of facilities for part-time, or adult, further education by the external institution in any academic year, and

(b) there are no arrangements for the provision in that year of any facilities of the kind specified in the application for the population of the sponsoring body's locality by any other institutions or the arrangements for such provision for that population in that year by other institutions are inadequate,

the sponsoring body shall apply to the council specified in the request for financial support to be given to the sponsoring body on terms requiring it to be applied in respect of the provision of the facilities specified in the application by the external institution in that year.

(6) In subsection (5) above—

(a) references to part-time, or adult, further education are to education provided by means of courses of any description mentioned in Schedule 2 to this Act, and

(b) references to the provision of facilities for such education by any institution in any academic year include the provision of facilities, and the carrying on of any activities, which the governing body of the institution consider necessary or desirable to be provided or carried on for the purpose of or in connection with the provision of facilities for such education by them in that year,

and that subsection applies to an institution within the further education sector if the institution is for the time being specified in an order, or for the time being falls within a description specified in an order, made by the Secretary of State.

**7.**—(1) The Secretary of State may make grants to each of the councils of such amounts and subject to such terms and conditions as he may determine.

(2) The terms and conditions subject to which grants are made by the Secretary of State to either of the councils—

    (a) may in particular impose requirements to be complied with in respect of every institution, or every institution falling within a class or description specified in the terms and conditions, being requirements to be complied with in the case of any institution to which the requirements apply before financial support of any amount or description so specified is provided by the council in respect of activities carried on by the institution, but

    (b) shall not otherwise relate to the provision of financial support by the council in respect of activities carried on by any particular institution or institutions.

(3) Such terms and conditions may in particular—

    (a) enable the Secretary of State to require the repayment, in whole or in part, of sums paid by him if any of the terms and conditions subject to which the sums were paid is not complied with, and

    (b) require the payment of interest in respect of any period during which a sum due to the Secretary of State in accordance with any of the terms and conditions remains unpaid.

### Further functions

**8.**—(1) Each council—

    (a) shall provide the Secretary of State with such information or advice relating to the provision for the population of their area of further education as he may from time to time require, and

    (b) may provide the Secretary of State with such information or advice relating to such provision as they think fit,

and information and advice provided under this subsection shall be provided in such manner as the Secretary of State may from time to time determine.

(2) Each council shall keep under review the matters in respect of which they have power under this Part of this Act to give financial support.

(3) Where in the case of an institution within the further education sector or which provides any facilities for further education, the Secretary of State has, before the date on which the councils were established, made any grant, loan or other payment to the institution subject to any terms or conditions—

    (a) all the functions of the Secretary of State in relation to the grant, loan or other payment shall, if the Secretary of State so directs, be exercisable on his behalf by a council in accordance with such directions as he may give from time to time,

    (b) the council shall keep the Secretary of State informed of any action they take or propose to take in the exercise of those functions, and

    (c) the council shall immediately pay to the Secretary of State any sums received by them in the exercise of those functions.

(4) The Secretary of State may by order confer or impose on a council such supplementary functions relating to the provision of education as he thinks fit.

(5) For the purposes of subsection (4) above a function is a supplementary function in relation to a council if it is exercisable for the purposes of—

(a) the exercise by the Secretary of State of functions of his under any enactment, or

(b) the doing by the Secretary of State of anything he has power to do apart from any enactment,

and it is relevant to the provision of facilities for further education for the population of the council's area.

Assessment of quality of education provided by institutions.

**9.**—(1) Each council shall—

(a) secure that provision is made for assessing the quality of education provided in institutions within the further education sector, and

(b) establish a committee, to be known as the "Quality Assessment Committee", with the function of giving them advice on the discharge of their duty under paragraph (a) above and such other functions as may be conferred on the committee by the council.

(2) The majority of the members of the committee—

(a) shall be persons falling within subsection (3) below, and

(b) shall not be members of the council.

(3) Persons fall within this subsection if they appear to the council to have experience of, and to have shown capacity in, the provision of further education and, in appointing such persons, the council shall have regard to the desirability of their being currently engaged in the provision of further education or in carrying responsibility for such provision.

(4) Her Majesty's Chief Inspector of Schools in Wales shall, if asked to do so by the Further Education Funding Council for Wales, assess the quality of education provided in any institutions within the further education sector or any other institutions for which the council give, or are considering giving, financial support under this Part of this Act.

(5) Schedule 1 to this Act shall apply to a committee established under this section as it applies to committees established under paragraph 8 of that Schedule.

*Adjustment of local education authority sector*

Functions of local education authorities in respect of secondary education.
1944 c. 31.

**10.**—(1) In section 8 of the Education Act 1944 (duties of local education authorities) for subsection (1)(b) (secondary education) there is substituted—

"(b) for providing full-time education suitable to the requirements of pupils of compulsory school age, being either senior pupils or junior pupils who have attained the age of ten years and six months and whom it is expedient to educate together with senior pupils of compulsory school age."

(2) After subsection (1) of that section there is inserted—

"(1A) A local education authority shall have power to secure the provision for their area of full-time education suitable to the requirements of persons over compulsory school age who have not attained the age of nineteen years, including provision for persons from other areas."

(3) In subsection (2) of that section (subsidiary obligations) for "fulfilling their duties" there is substituted "exercising their functions".

**11.** For section 41 of the Education Act 1944 (functions of local education authorities in respect of further education) there is substituted—

*Functions of local education authorities in respect of further education.*

Functions of local education authorities in respect of further education.
1944 c. 31.

41.—(1) It shall be the duty of every local education authority to secure the provision for their area of adequate facilities for further education.

(2) Subsection (1) above does not apply to education to which section 2(1) or 3(1) of the Further and Higher Education Act 1992 applies, but in respect of education to which section 3(1) of that Act applies a local education authority may—

(a) secure the provision for their area of such facilities as appear to them to be appropriate for meeting the needs of the population of their area; and

(b) do anything which appears to them to be necessary or expedient for the purposes of or in connection with such provision.

(3) Subject to subsection (4) below and section 14(1) to (4) of the Further and Higher Education Act 1992, in this Act "further education" means—

(a) full-time and part-time education suitable to the requirements of persons over compulsory school age (including vocational, social, physical and recreational training); and

(b) organized leisure-time occupation provided in connection with the provision of such education.

(4) In this Act "further education" does not include higher education or secondary education.

(5) In subsection (3)(b) above "organized leisure time occupation" means leisure-time occupation, in such organized cultural training and recreative activities as are suited to their requirements, for any persons over compulsory school age who are able and willing to profit by facilities provided for that purpose.

(6) A local education authority may secure the provision of further education for persons from other areas.

(7) In exercising their functions under this section a local education authority shall have regard to any educational facilities provided by institutions within the higher education sector or the further education sector, and other bodies, which are provided for, or available for use by persons in, their area.

(8) In exercising their functions under this section a local education authority shall also have regard to the requirements of persons over compulsory school age who have learning difficulties.

(9) Subject to subsection (10) below, for the purposes of subsection (8) above a person has a "learning difficulty" if—

    (a) he has a significantly greater difficulty in learning than the majority of persons of his age; or

    (b) he has a disability which either prevents or hinders him from making use of facilities of a kind generally provided in pursuance of the duty under subsection (1) above for persons of his age.

(10) A person is not to be taken as having a learning difficulty solely because the language (or form of the language) in which he is, or will be, taught is different from a language (or form of a language) which has at any time been spoken in his home.

(11) A local education authority may do anything which appears to them to be necessary or expedient for the purposes of or in connection with the exercise of their functions under this section."

*Provision of further education in schools*

Provision of further education in maintained schools.
1944 c. 31.

**12.**—(1) At the end of section 9 of the Education Act 1944 (power of local authority to establish schools) there is added—

"(7) The powers conferred by subsection (1) of this section shall not extend to establishing a school to provide—

    (a) part-time education suitable to the requirements of persons of any age over compulsory school age; or

    (b) full-time education suitable to the requirements of persons who have attained the age of nineteen years".

1980 c. 20.

(2) In section 13 of the Education Act 1980 (requirement to publish proposal for alteration of voluntary school) after subsection (1) there is inserted—

"(1A) The reference in subsection (1) above to a change in the character of a school does not include a change in character resulting only from persons beginning or ceasing to be provided with—

    (a) part-time education suitable to the requirements of persons of any age over compulsory school age; or

(b) full-time education suitable to the requirements of persons who have attained the age of nineteen years;

and no proposals under this section by any persons that a school established or proposed to be established by them, or by persons whom they represent, should be maintained by a local education authority shall be approved by the Secretary of State if the school or proposed school is to provide education falling within paragraph (a) or (b) above".

(3) In Part III of the Education (No. 2) Act 1986 (conduct of county, voluntary and maintained special schools) after section 16 there is inserted—

1986 c. 61.

"Provision of further education.

16A.—(1) The governing body of any county, voluntary or maintained special school shall be responsible for determining whether or not to provide—

(a) part-time education suitable to the requirements of persons of any age over compulsory school age; or

(b) full-time education suitable to the requirements of persons who have attained the age of nineteen years,

but the governing body of a maintained special school shall not determine to provide, or to cease to provide, such education without the consent of the local education authority.

(2) It shall be the duty of the governing body of any such school which provides such education to secure that such education is not provided at any time in a room where pupils are at that time being taught except in such circumstances as may be prescribed."

(4) In section 9 of the Education Reform Act 1988 (exceptions, etc, relating to religious education for pupils) after subsection (1) there is inserted—

1988 c. 40.

"(1A) It shall not be required, as a condition of any person attending any maintained school to receive further education, that he shall attend or abstain from attending any Sunday school or any place of religious worship."

(5) In section 33 of that Act (schemes for financing schools), in subsection (4)(a) (meaning of general schools budget) after "that authority" there is inserted "(other than expenditure in respect of the provision of part-time education suitable to the requirements of persons of any age over compulsory school age or full-time education suitable to the requirements of persons who have attained the age of nineteen years)".

(6) In section 36 of that Act (delegation to governing body of management of school's budget share), after subsection (5) (governing body entitled to spend sums for the purposes of the school) there is inserted—

"(5A) In subsection (5) above "the purposes of the school" does not include purposes wholly referable to the provision of—

>   (a) part-time education suitable to the requirements of persons of any age over compulsory school age; or
>
>   (b) full-time education suitable to the requirements of persons who have attained the age of nineteen years".

(7) In section 38 of that Act (determination of budget share), after subsection (3) (matters that must or may be taken into account) there is inserted—

>   "(3A) The allocation formula under a scheme shall not include provision for taking into account persons provided with—
>
>   (a) part-time education suitable to the requirements of persons of any age over compulsory school age; or
>
>   (b) full-time education suitable to the requirements of persons who have attained the age of nineteen years".

(8) In section 105 of that Act (city technology colleges etc.), in subsection (2)(b) (must provide education for pupils who have attained eleven but not nineteen years) "but not the age of nineteen years" is omitted.

(9) In section 106 of that Act (prohibition of charges), after subsection (1) (no charges for admission to maintained school) there is inserted—

>   "(1A) Subsection (1) above shall not apply to the admission of any person to any maintained school for the purpose of—
>
>   (a) part-time education suitable to the requirements of persons of any age over compulsory school age; or
>
>   (b) full-time education suitable to the requirements of persons who have attained the age of nineteen years".

Provision of further education in grant-maintained schools.
1988 c. 40.

**13.**—(1) In section 57(5) of the Education Reform Act 1988 (provision by grant-maintained school of education which is neither primary nor secondary) after "provided that" there is inserted—

>   "(a) it is part-time education suitable to the requirements of persons of any age over compulsory school age, or full-time education suitable to the requirements of persons who have attained the age of nineteen years; or
>
>   (b)".

(2) At the end of section 79 of that Act (grants to grant-maintained schools in respect of expenditure for the purposes of the school) there is added—

>   "(13) In this section "the purposes of the school" do not include purposes wholly referable to the provision of—
>
>   (a) part-time education suitable to the requirements of persons of any age over compulsory school age; or
>
>   (b) full-time education suitable to the requirements of persons who have attained the age of nineteen years".

(3) In section 89 of that Act (change of character of grant-maintained school) after subsection (1) there is inserted—

"(1A) The reference in subsection (1) above to a change in the character of a school does not include a change in character resulting only from persons beginning or ceasing to be provided with part-time education suitable to the requirements of persons of any age over compulsory school age or full-time education suitable to the requirements of persons who have attained the age of nineteen years, but it shall be the duty of the governing body of any grant-maintained school which provides such education to secure that it is not provided at any time in a room where pupils are at that time being taught except in such circumstances as may be prescribed."

## General

**14.**—(1) Subject to subsection (2) below, for the purposes of the Education Acts education to which this subsection applies, that is, full-time education suitable to the requirements of persons over compulsory school age who have not attained the age of nineteen years, is further education not secondary education.

(2) Subject to subsection (3) below, for the purposes of those Acts—

    (a) education falling within section 8(1)(b) of the Education Act 1944 (full-time education suitable to the requirements of pupils of compulsory school age), and

    (b) education to which subsection (1) above applies provided at a school where education falling within section 8(1)(b) of that Act is also provided,

is secondary education not further education.

(3) For the purposes of the Education Acts education provided for persons who have attained the age of nineteen years is further education not secondary education; but where a person has begun a particular course of secondary education before attaining the age of eighteen years, then, if he continues to attend that course, the education does not cease to be secondary education by reason of his having attained the age of nineteen years.

(4) In subsections (1) to (3) above "education" does not include higher education.

(5) For the purposes of the Education Acts "school" means an educational institution not within the further education sector or the higher education sector, being an institution for providing any one or more of the following—

    (a) primary education,

    (b) education which is secondary education by virtue of subsection (2)(a) above, or

    (c) education to which subsection (1) above applies,

whether or not the institution also provides further education or other secondary education.

(6) For the purposes of the Education Acts, and of any instrument made or having effect as if made under those Acts, "pupil" means a person for whom education is being provided at a school, other than—

    (a) a person who has attained the age of nineteen years for whom further education is being provided, or

*(marginal notes:)*

Meaning of "further education", "secondary education", "school" and "pupil".

1944 c. 31.

PART I

(b) a person for whom part-time education suitable to the requirements of persons of any age over compulsory school age is being provided.

## CHAPTER II

### INSTITUTIONS WITHIN THE FURTHER EDUCATION SECTOR

#### *The further education corporations*

Initial
incorporation of
existing
institutions.

**15.**—(1) Before the appointed day the Secretary of State shall by order specify—

(a) each educational institution maintained by a local education authority which appears to him to fall within subsection (2) below, and

(b) each county school, controlled school or grant-maintained school which appears to him to fall within subsection (3) below.

(2) An institution falls within this subsection if on 1st November 1990 its enrolment number calculated in accordance with paragraph 1(1) of Schedule 3 to this Act was not less than 15 per cent. of its total enrolment number calculated in accordance with paragraph 1(2) of that Schedule.

(3) An institution falls within this subsection if on 17th January 1991 not less than 60 per cent. of the pupils at the institution were receiving full-time education suitable to the requirements of persons over compulsory school age who have not attained the age of nineteen years.

(4) On the appointed day a body corporate shall be established, for each institution so specified, for the purpose of conducting the institution as from the operative date.

(5) The name given in the order under subsection (1) above as the name of the institution shall be the initial name of the body corporate.

(6) Where an educational institution, being an institution maintained by a local education authority or a grant-maintained school, has been established since 1st November 1990 or, as the case may be, 17th January 1991 by a merger of two or more institutions existing on that date, the institution shall be treated as falling within subsection (2) or, as the case may be, subsection (3) above if it would have done so if the merger had taken place before that date.

(7) In this section "the appointed day" means the day appointed under section 94 of this Act for the commencement of subsection (4) above.

Orders
incorporating
further
institutions.

**16.**—(1) The Secretary of State may by order make provision for the establishment of a body corporate—

(a) for the purpose of establishing and conducting an educational institution, or

(b) for the purpose of conducting an existing educational institution,

but shall not make an order in respect of an existing institution without the consent of the governing body.

(2) Subsection (1) above does not apply to any educational institution maintained by a local education authority or any grant-maintained school; but if at any time it appears to the Secretary of State, in the case of any educational institution so maintained or any grant-maintained school—

    (a) that its enrolment number calculated in accordance with paragraph 1(1) of Schedule 3 to this Act was not less than 15 per cent. of its total enrolment number calculated in accordance with paragraph 1(2) of that Schedule, or

    (b) that it is principally concerned with the provision of full-time education suitable to the requirements of persons over compulsory school age who have not attained the age of nineteen years,

he may by order make provision for the establishment of a body corporate for the purpose of conducting that institution.

(3) If at any time a council proposes to the Secretary of State that a body corporate should be established for the purpose of conducting an educational institution which—

    (a) is maintained by a local education authority or is a grant-maintained school, and

    (b) is principally concerned with the provision of further or higher education or full-time education suitable to the requirements of persons over compulsory school age who have not attained the age of nineteen years,

the Secretary of State may by order make provision for the establishment of a body corporate for that purpose.

(4) The name given in the order under this section as the name of the institution shall be the initial name of the body corporate.

(5) An order under this section shall provide for the institution to be conducted by the body corporate as from the operative date.

**17.**—(1) In this Act "further education corporation" means a body corporate established under section 15 or 16 of this Act.

(2) In this Part of this Act "operative date", in relation to a further education corporation and the institution, means—

    (a) in the case of a further education corporation established under section 15 of this Act, such date as the Secretary of State may by order appoint in relation to the corporations so established, and

    (b) in the case of a further education corporation established under section 16 of this Act, such date as the Secretary of State may by order appoint in relation to that corporation.

*"Further education corporation" and "operative date".*

**18.**—(1) A further education corporation may—

    (a) provide further and higher education, and

    (b) supply goods or services in connection with their provision of education,

and those powers are referred to in section 19 of this Act as the corporation's principal powers.

*Principal powers of a further education corporation.*

(2) For the purposes of subsection (1) above, goods are supplied in connection with the provision of education by a further education corporation if they result from—

(a) their provision of education or anything done by them under this Act for the purpose of or in connection with their provision of education,

(b) the use of their facilities or the expertise of persons employed by them in the fields in which they are so employed, or

(c) ideas of a person employed by them, or of one of their students, arising out of their provision of education.

(3) For the purposes of that subsection, services are supplied in connection with the provision of education by a further education corporation if—

(a) they result from their provision of education or anything done by them under this Act for the purpose of or in connection with their provision of education,

(b) they are provided by making available their facilities or the expertise of persons employed by them in the fields in which they are so employed, or

(c) they result from ideas of a person employed by them, or of one of their students, arising out of their provision of education.

Supplementary powers of a further education corporation.

**19.**—(1) A further education corporation may do anything (including in particular the things referred to in subsections (2) to (4) below) which appears to the corporation to be necessary or expedient for the purpose of or in connection with the exercise of any of their principal powers.

(2) A further education corporation may conduct an educational institution for the purpose of carrying on activities undertaken in the exercise of their powers to provide further or higher education and, in particular, may assume as from the operative date the conduct of the institution in respect of which the corporation is established.

(3) A further education corporation may provide facilities of any description appearing to the corporation to be necessary or desirable for the purposes of or in connection with carrying on any activities undertaken in the exercise of their principal powers (including boarding accommodation and recreational facilities for students and staff and facilities to meet the needs of students having learning difficulties within the meaning of section 4(6) of this Act).

(4) A further education corporation may—

(a) acquire and dispose of land and other property,

(b) enter into contracts, including in particular—

(i) contracts for the employment of teachers and other staff for the purposes of or in connection with carrying on any activities undertaken in the exercise of their principal powers, and

(ii) contracts with respect to the carrying on by the corporation of any such activities,

(c) borrow such sums as the corporation think fit for the purposes of carrying on any activities they have power to carry on or meeting any liability transferred to them under sections 23 to 27 of this Act and, in connection with such borrowing, may grant any mortgage, charge or other security in respect of any land or other property of the corporation,

(d) invest any sums not immediately required for the purposes of carrying on any activities they have power to carry on,

(e) accept gifts of money, land or other property and apply it, or hold and administer it on trust for, any of those purposes, and

(f) do anything incidental to the conduct of an educational institution providing further or higher education, including founding scholarships or exhibitions, making grants and giving prizes.

(5) The power conferred on a further education corporation by subsection (4)(c) above to borrow money may not be exercised without the consent of the appropriate council, and such consent may be given for particular borrowing or for borrowing of a particular class.

**20.**—(1) For every further education corporation established to conduct an educational institution there shall be—

(a) an instrument providing for the constitution of the corporation (to be known as the instrument of government), and

(b) an instrument in accordance with which the corporation, and the institution, are to be conducted (to be known as articles of government).

Constitution of corporation and conduct of the institution.

(2) Instruments of government and articles of government—

(a) shall comply with the requirements of Schedule 4 to this Act, and

(b) may make any provision authorised to be made by that Schedule and such other provision as may be necessary or desirable.

(3) The validity of any proceedings of a further education corporation, or of any committee of the corporation, shall not be affected by a vacancy amongst the members or by any defect in the appointment or nomination of a member.

(4) Every document purporting to be an instrument made or issued by or on behalf of a further education corporation and to be duly executed under the seal of the corporation, or to be signed or executed by a person authorised by the corporation to act in that behalf, shall be received in evidence and be treated, without further proof, as being so made or issued unless the contrary is shown.

**21.**—(1) As from the date on which a further education corporation is established, the instrument of government and articles of government—

Initial instruments and articles.

(a) in the case of an institution which was a grant-maintained school on that date, shall be such as is prescribed by the order in respect of the institution under section 15 or 16 of this Act, and

(b) in any other case, shall be such as is prescribed by regulations.

PART I

(2) Such orders and regulations—

    (a) may provide for all or any of the persons who, on the date on which a corporation is established to conduct the grant-maintained school or other existing institution, are the members of the governing body of the institution to be the initial members of the corporation, and

    (b) may make such other provision in relation to grant-maintained schools or other existing institutions as appears to the Secretary of State necessary or desirable to secure continuity in their government.

(3) In the case of a further education corporation established to conduct an institution which, on the date the corporation was established, was a grant-maintained school, the governing body incorporated under Chapter IV of Part I of the Education Reform Act 1988 shall, on the operative date, be dissolved.

1988 c. 40.

Subsequent instruments and articles.

**22.**—(1) The Secretary of State may, after consulting the appropriate council—

    (a) if a further education corporation submits a draft of an instrument of government to have effect in place of their existing instrument, by order make a new instrument of government in terms of the draft or in such terms as he thinks fit, and

    (b) if such a corporation submits draft modifications of an instrument made under paragraph (a) above, by order modify the instrument in terms of the draft or in such terms as he thinks fit,

but shall not make a new instrument otherwise than in terms of the draft, or modify the instrument otherwise than in terms of the draft, unless he has consulted the corporation.

(2) The Secretary of State may by order modify any instrument of government of any further education corporation.

(3) An order under subsection (2) above—

    (a) may relate to all further education corporations, to any category of such corporations specified in the order or to any such corporation so specified, but

    (b) shall not be made unless the Secretary of State has consulted the appropriate council and each further education corporation to which the order relates.

(4) A further education corporation may, with the consent of the Secretary of State—

    (a) make new articles of government in place of their existing articles, or

    (b) modify their existing articles.

(5) The Secretary of State may by a direction under this section require further education corporations, any class of such corporations specified in the direction or any particular further education corporation so specified—

    (a) to modify their articles of government, or

(b) to secure that any rules or bye-laws made in pursuance of their articles of government are modified,

in any manner so specified.

(6) Before giving a direction under this section, the Secretary of State shall consult the further education corporation or (as the case may be) each further education corporation to which the direction applies.

### *Transfer of property, etc., to further education corporations*

**23.**—(1) This section has effect in relation to a further education corporation established to conduct an institution which, on the date the corporation was established, was maintained by a local education authority.

Transfer of property, etc.: institutions maintained by local education authorities.

(2) Subject to subsection (3) below and section 36 of this Act, on the operative date—

(a) all land or other property which, immediately before that date, was property of any local authority used or held for the purposes of the institution the corporation is established to conduct, and

(b) all rights and liabilities of any such authority subsisting immediately before that date which were acquired or incurred for those purposes,

shall be transferred to, and by virtue of this Act vest in, that corporation.

(3) Subsection (2) above shall not apply to—

(a) any liability of any such authority in respect of the principal of, or interest on, any loan, or

(b) any property, rights or liabilities excluded under subsections (4) or (5) below.

(4) If before the operative date—

(a) the governing body of the institution and the local authority have agreed in writing to exclude any land, and

(b) the Secretary of State has given his written approval of the agreement,

the land, and any rights or liabilities relating to it, shall be excluded.

(5) If in default of agreement under subsection (4) above—

(a) the governing body or the local authority have applied to the Secretary of State to exclude any land, and

(b) the Secretary of State has by order directed its exclusion,

the land, and any rights or liabilities relating to it, shall be excluded.

(6) An agreement under subsection (4) above may provide for the land to be used for the purposes of the institution on such terms as may be specified in or determined in accordance with the agreement; and directions under subsection (5) above—

(a) may confer any rights or impose any liabilities that could have been conferred or imposed by such an agreement, and

(b) shall have effect as if contained in such an agreement.

(7) References in subsections (4) and (5) above to anything done, other than the making of an order, include anything done before the passing of this Act.

(8) On the operative date—

(a) all land and other property which, immediately before that date, was property of the former governing body, and

(b) all rights and liabilities of that body subsisting immediately before that date,

shall be transferred to and, by virtue of this Act, vest in the corporation.

(9) In subsection (8) above "former governing body" in relation to an institution means the governing body of the institution immediately before the operative date.

Provisions supplementary to section 23.
1985 c. 47.

**24.**—(1) Where in exercise of their powers under section 2 of the Further Education Act 1985 a local authority—

(a) have entered into an agreement for the supply of goods or services or both through an educational institution, or

(b) for the purposes of any agreement for such a supply through such an institution, hold shares in any body corporate,

and a further education corporation is established to conduct the institution, then, the rights and liabilities of the authority under or by virtue of the agreement or, as the case may be, the interest of the authority in the shares shall be treated as falling within section 23(2) of this Act.

(2) Expressions used in subsection (1) above and in section 2 of that Act have the same meaning as in that section.

(3) Where, immediately before the operative date in relation to a further education corporation, arrangements exist for the supply by a local authority of goods or services for the purposes of the institution in pursuance of a bid prepared under section 7 of the Local Government Act 1988 (restrictions on activities of local authorities), those arrangements shall have effect as from that date as if—

1988 c. 9.

(a) they were contained in an agreement made before that date between the local authority and the corporation on the terms specified in the bid, and

(b) the agreement required the corporation or, as the case may be, the local authority to make payments corresponding to the provision made in the bid in pursuance of section 8(3) of that Act for items to be credited or, as the case may be, debited to any account.

(4) Where such arrangements are for the supply to others as well as to the institution—

(a) those arrangements shall have effect as mentioned in subsection (3) above only to the extent that they relate to the institution in question, and

(b) the rights and liabilities arising under the agreement shall be such rights and liabilities as are properly required to give effect to the arrangements so far as relating to that institution.

(5) Where at any time land is used for the purposes of such an institution, any interest of a local authority in the land subsisting at that time shall be taken for the purposes of section 23 of this Act to be land held for the purposes of that institution (whether or not it is by virtue of that interest that the land is so used).

**25.**—(1) This section has effect in relation to a further education corporation established to conduct an institution which, on the date the corporation was established, was a grant-maintained school.

(2) On the operative date—

(a) all land or other property which, immediately before that date, was property of the governing body, and

(b) all rights and liabilities of that body subsisting immediately before that date,

shall be transferred to and, by virtue of this Act, vest in the corporation.

**26.**—(1) This section applies to any person who immediately before the operative date in relation to a further education corporation established to conduct an institution which, on the date the corporation was established, was maintained by a local education authority or was a grant-maintained school—

(a) is employed by the transferor to work solely at the institution the corporation is established to conduct, or

(b) is employed by the transferor to work at that institution and is designated for the purposes of this section by an order made by the Secretary of State.

(2) A contract of employment between a person to whom this section applies and the transferor shall have effect from the operative date as if originally made between that person and the corporation.

(3) Without prejudice to subsection (2) above—

(a) all the transferor's rights, powers, duties and liabilities under or in connection with a contract to which that subsection applies shall by virtue of this section be transferred to the corporation on the operative date, and

(b) anything done before that date by or in relation to the transferor in respect of that contract or the employee shall be deemed from that date to have been done by or in relation to the corporation.

(4) Subsections (2) and (3) above are without prejudice to any right of an employee to terminate his contract of employment if a substantial change is made to his detriment in his working conditions, but no such right shall arise by reason only of the change in employer effected by this section.

(5) An order under this section may designate a person either individually or as a member of a class or description of employees.

(6) References in this section, in relation to a further education corporation, to the transferor are—

(a) in relation to a corporation established to conduct an institution which, on the date on which it was established, was maintained by a local education authority, that authority,

     (b) in relation to a corporation established to conduct an institution which, on that date, was a voluntary aided or special agreement school, the governing body of the school, and

     (c) in relation to a corporation established to conduct an institution which, on that date, was a grant-maintained school, the governing body of the school.

(7) For the purposes of this section—

     (a) a person employed by the transferor is to be regarded as employed to work at an institution if his employment with the transferor for the time being involves work at that institution, and

     (b) subject to subsection (8) below, a person employed by the transferor is to be regarded as employed to work solely at an institution if his only employment with the transferor (disregarding any employment under a separate contract with the transferor) is for the time being at that institution.

(8) A person employed by the transferor in connection with the provision of meals shall not be regarded for the purposes of subsection (7)(b) above as employed to work solely at an institution unless the meals are provided solely for consumption by persons at the institution.

(9) This section is subject to section 48 of this Act.

*Dissolution of further education corporations*

Dissolution of further education corporations.

**27.**—(1) Subject to the following provisions of this section, the Secretary of State may by order provide for the dissolution of any further education corporation and the transfer to any person mentioned in subsection (2) or (3) below of property, rights and liabilities of the corporation.

(2) Such property, rights and liabilities may be transferred to—

     (a) any person appearing to the Secretary of State to be wholly or mainly engaged in the provision of educational facilities or services of any description, or

     (b) any body corporate established for purposes which include the provision of such facilities or services,

with the consent of the person or body in question.

(3) Such property, rights and liabilities may be transferred to—

     (a) a council, or

     (b) a higher education funding council.

(4) Where the recipient of a transfer under any order under this section is not a charity established for charitable purposes which are exclusively educational purposes, any property transferred must be transferred on trust to be used for charitable purposes which are exclusively educational purposes.

1960 c. 58.

(5) In subsection (4) above "charity" and "charitable purposes" have the same meanings as in the Charities Act 1960.

(6) An order under this section may apply section 26 of this Act with such modifications as the Secretary of State may consider necessary or desirable.

(7) Before making an order under this section in respect of a further education corporation the Secretary of State shall consult—

    (a) the corporation, and

    (b) the appropriate council, unless the order was made for the purpose of giving effect to a proposal of that council.

*Designation of institutions for funding by the councils*

**28.**—(1) The Secretary of State may by order designate as eligible to receive support from funds administered by the councils any educational institution principally concerned with the provision of one or both of the following—

    (a) full-time education suitable to the requirements of persons over compulsory school age who have not attained the age of nineteen years, and

    (b) courses of further or higher education,

if the institution meets the requirements of subsection (2) below.

Designation of institutions.

(2) The institution must be one of the following—

    (a) a voluntary aided school,

    (b) an institution (other than a school) assisted by a local education authority, or

    (c) an institution which is grant-aided or eligible to receive aid by way of grant.

(3) For the purposes of subsection (2)(c) above an institution is grant-aided or eligible to receive aid by way of grant if it is maintained by persons other than local education authorities who—

    (a) receive any grants under regulations made under section 100(1)(b) of the Education Act 1944, or

    (b) are eligible to receive such grants.

1944 c. 31.

(4) In this Part of this Act "designated institution" means an institution in relation to which a designation under this section has effect.

**29.**—(1) This section has effect in relation to any designated institution, other than—

    (a) an institution conducted by a company, or

    (b) an institution conducted by an unincorporated association if the order designating the institution provides for its exemption.

Government and conduct of designated institutions.

(2) For each institution in relation to which this section has effect there shall be—

    (a) an instrument providing for the constitution of a governing body of the institution (to be known as the instrument of government), and

    (b) an instrument in accordance with which the institution is to be conducted (to be known as the articles of government),

each of which meets the requirements of subsection (3) below.

(3) Those requirements are that the instrument—

    (a) was in force when the designation took effect and is approved for the purposes of this section by the Secretary of State,

(b) is made in pursuance of a power under a regulatory instrument, or is made under subsection (5) below, and is approved for the purposes of this section by the Secretary of State, or

(c) is made under subsection (6) below.

(4) In this section "regulatory instrument", in relation to an institution, means any instrument of government or articles of government and any other instrument relating to or regulating the institution.

(5) Where there is no such power as is mentioned in subsection (3)(b) above to make the instrument, it may be made by the governing body of the institution and an instrument made by them under this subsection may replace wholly or partly any existing regulatory instrument.

(6) The Secretary of State may by order make either of the instruments referred to in subsection (2) above and any instrument made by him under this subsection may replace wholly or partly any existing regulatory instrument.

(7) If an instrument approved by the Secretary of State for the purposes of this section—

(a) falls within subsection (3)(a) above or was made in pursuance of a power under a regulatory instrument and, apart from this section, there is no power to modify it, or

(b) was made by the governing body of the institution,

the instrument may be modified by the governing body.

(8) The Secretary of State may by order modify either of the instruments referred to in subsection (2) above and no instrument approved by him for the purposes of this section may be modified by any other person without the Secretary of State's consent.

(9) Before exercising any power under subsection (6) or (8) above in relation to any instrument the Secretary of State shall consult—

(a) the governing body of the institution, and

(b) where there is such a power as is mentioned in subsection (3)(b) above to make or, as the case may be, modify the instrument and the persons having that power are different from the governing body of the institution, the persons having the power,

so far as it appears to him to be practicable to do so.

Special provision for voluntary aided sixth form colleges.

**30.** Notwithstanding anything in section 29 of this Act, the instrument of government of an institution which, when designated, was a voluntary aided school must provide—

(a) for the governing body of the institution to include persons appointed for the purpose of securing so far as practicable that the established character of the institution at the time of its designation is preserved and developed and, in particular, that the school is conducted in accordance with any trust deed relating to it, and

(b) for the majority of members of the governing body to be such governors.

**31.**—(1) This section has effect in relation to any designated institution conducted by a company.

(2) The articles of association of the company shall incorporate—

(a) provision with respect to the constitution of a governing body of the institution (to be known as the instrument of government of the institution), and

(b) provision with respect to the conduct of the institution (to be known as the articles of government of the institution).

(3) The Secretary of State may give to the persons who appear to him to have effective control over the company such directions as he thinks fit for securing that—

(a) the memorandum or articles of association of the company, or

(b) any rules or bye-laws made in pursuance of any power conferred by the articles of association of the company,

are amended in such manner as he may specify in the direction.

(4) No amendment of the memorandum or articles of association of the company (other than one required under subsection (3)(a) above) shall take effect until it has been submitted to the Secretary of State for his approval and he has notified his approval to the company.

(5) Before giving any directions under subsection (3) above the Secretary of State shall consult the persons who appear to him to have effective control over the company.

**32.**—(1) This section has effect in relation to an institution designated under section 28 of this Act in any case where—

(a) the order designating the institution under that section so provides, and

(b) when designated the institution was a voluntary aided school or an institution (other than a school) assisted by a local education authority.

(2) Subject to subsection (4) below and section 36 of this Act, on the designation date—

(a) all land or other property which, immediately before that date, was property of a former assisting authority used or held for the purposes of the institution, and

(b) all rights and liabilities of that authority subsisting immediately before that date which were acquired or incurred for those purposes,

shall be transferred to and, by virtue of this Act, vest in the appropriate transferees.

(3) In this section and section 33 of this Act—

"appropriate transferees" means—

(a) in relation to an institution conducted by a company, the company, and

(b) in relation to an institution not so conducted, any persons specified in the order designating the institution as persons appearing to the Secretary of State to be trustees holding property for the purposes of that institution, "designation date", in relation to a designated institution, means the date on which the designation takes effect, and

"former assisting authority" means—

(a) in relation to an institution which when designated was a voluntary aided school, the local education authority which maintained the school, and

(b) in relation to an institution which when designated was an institution (other than a school) assisted by a local education authority, that authority.

(4) Subsection (2) above shall not apply to—

(a) any liability of a former assisting authority in respect of the principal of, or interest on, any loan, or

(b) any property, rights or liabilities excluded under subsections (5) or (6) below.

(5) If before the designation date—

(a) the appropriate transferees and the former assisting authority have agreed in writing to exclude any land, and

(b) the Secretary of State has given his written approval of the agreement,

the land, and any rights or liabilities relating to it, shall be excluded.

(6) If in default of agreement under subsection (5) above—

(a) the appropriate transferees or the former assisting authority have applied to the Secretary of State to exclude any land, and

(b) the Secretary of State has by order directed its exclusion,

the land, and any rights or liabilities relating to it, shall be excluded.

(7) An agreement under subsection (5) above may provide for the land to be used for the purposes of the institution on such terms as may be specified in or determined in accordance with the agreement; and directions under subsection (6) above—

(a) may confer any rights or impose any liabilities that could have been conferred or imposed by such an agreement, and

(b) shall have effect as if contained in such an agreement.

(8) References in subsections (5) and (6) above to anything done, other than the making of an order, include anything done before the passing of this Act.

Provisions supplementary to section 32.

**33.**—(1) Subject to section 36(2) of this Act, where persons appearing to the Secretary of State to be trustees holding property for the purposes of the institution are the appropriate transferee, any land or other property or rights transferred to them under section 32 of this Act shall be held on the trusts applicable under such trust deed relating to or regulating that institution (if any) as may be specified in the order designating the institution or, if no such trust deed is so specified, on trust for the general purposes of the institution.

(2) Where persons so appearing to the Secretary of State are the appropriate transferee, they shall incur no personal liability by virtue of any liability so transferred but may apply any property held by them on trust for the purposes of the institution in meeting any such liability.

(3) Where at any time land is used for the purposes of an institution, any interest of a local authority in the land subsisting at that time shall be taken for the purposes of that section to be land held for the purposes of that institution (whether or not it is by virtue of that interest that the land is so used).

(4) References in this Part of this Act to the operative date, in relation to a designated institution, are to the designation date.

### *Property, rights and liabilities: general*

**34.**—(1) The Secretary of State may by order provide for any land or other property of a local authority to be made available for use by an institution within the further education sector (referred to in this section as the "new sector institution") if the requirements of subsection (2) below are satisfied.

Making additional property available for use.

(2) Those requirements are that in the opinion of the Secretary of State—

(a) the property—

(i) either has within the preceding six months been used for the purpose of the provision of further education by an institution maintained by a local education authority but its use for that purpose has been discontinued or the local education authority intend its use for that purpose to be discontinued, or

(ii) is being used for that purpose but the local education authority intend its use for that purpose to be discontinued, and

(b) it is necessary or desirable for the property to be available for use for the purposes of the new sector institution but the governing body of that institution have been unable to secure agreement with the local authority, on such terms as may reasonably be required, to secure that the property is so available.

(3) The Secretary of State shall not make an order under this section unless—

(a) the governing body of the new sector institution have applied to him, before the end of the period of three years beginning with the date which is the operative date in relation to further education corporations established under section 15 of this Act, for such an order to be made, and

(b) he has consulted the appropriate council, the local authority and the Education Assets Board.

(4) For the purpose of making any property available for use for the purposes of an institution, an order under this section may—

(a) transfer to, and vest in, the governing body—

(i) the property concerned, and

(ii) any rights or liabilities of the local authority acquired or incurred for the purpose of the provision of further education there, or

(b) confer any rights or impose any liabilities and, to the extent (if any) that the order does so, it shall have effect as if contained in an agreement between the local authority and the governing body.

(5) Subsection (4)(a)(ii) above shall not apply to any liability of the local authority in respect of the principal of, or interest on, any loan.

(6) References in this section to use for the purpose of the provision of further education are to use wholly or mainly for that purpose.

Voluntary transfers of staff in connection with section 34.

**35.**—(1) This section applies where—

(a) for the purpose of making any property of a local authority available for use for the purposes of an institution within the further education sector, an order is made under section 34 of this Act,

(b) at any time on or after such date as may be specified by the order a person employed by the local authority ceases to be so employed and is subsequently employed by the governing body of the institution, and

1978 c. 44.

(c) by virtue of section 84 of the Employment Protection (Consolidation) Act 1978 (renewal or re-engagement) that subsequent employment precludes his receiving any redundancy payment under Part VI of that Act.

(2) Schedule 13 to that Act (computation of period of employment for the purposes of that Act) shall have effect in relation to that person as if it included the following provisions—

(a) the period of employment of that person with the local authority shall count as a period of employment with the governing body, and

(b) the change of employer shall not break the continuity of the period of employment.

(3) The period of that person's employment with the local authority shall count as a period of employment with the governing body for the purposes of any provision of his contract of employment with the governing body which depends on his length of service with that employer.

General provisions about transfers under Chapter II.

**36.**—(1) This section applies to any transfer under section 23 or 32 of this Act, and those sections are subject to Schedule 5 to this Act.

(2) Where any land or other property or rights—

(a) were immediately before the operative date in relation to any institution held on trust for any particular purposes, or (as the case may be) for the general purposes, of the institution, and

(b) fall to be transferred under any transfer to which this section applies,

they shall continue to be so held by the transferee.

(3) Schedule 5 to this Act has effect for the purpose of—

  (a) dividing and apportioning property, rights and liabilities which fall to be transferred under any transfer to which this section applies where that property has been used or held, or the rights or liabilities have been acquired or incurred, for the purposes of more than one educational institution,

  (b) excluding from transfer in certain circumstances property, rights and liabilities which would otherwise fall to be transferred under any such transfer,

  (c) providing for identifying and defining the property, rights and liabilities which fall to be so transferred, and

  (d) making supplementary and consequential provisions in relation to transfers to which this section applies.

(4) Where arrangements for the supply by a local authority of goods or services for the purposes of an institution to be conducted by a further education corporation are to have effect as from the operative date in accordance with section 24(4) of this Act as if contained in an agreement made before that date between the local authority and the corporation, paragraphs 2 to 5 of Schedule 5 to this Act shall have effect as if the rights and liabilities of the corporation under the agreement were rights and liabilities of the local authority transferred to the corporation under a transfer to which this section applies.

(5) In carrying out the functions conferred or imposed on them by that Schedule, it shall be the duty of the Education Assets Board to secure that each transfer to which this section applies is, so far as practicable, fully effective on the date on which it takes effect under this Act.

(6) Where in accordance with that Schedule anything falls to be or may be done by the Board for the purposes of or in connection with any such transfer—

  (a) it may not be done by the transferee, and

  (b) in doing it the Board shall be regarded as acting on behalf and in the name of the transferee,

and in a case where the transferee is a body corporate established under this Act paragraph (b) above applies both in relation to things done before and in relation to things done after that body is established under this Act.

(7) Not later than the end of the period of six months beginning with the operative date in relation to a further education corporation established under section 15 of this Act, the Board shall provide the appropriate council with a written statement giving such particulars of all property, rights and liabilities transferred to that corporation as are then available to the Board.

(8) If in any case within subsection (7) above full particulars of all property, rights and liabilities transferred to the corporation concerned are not given in the statement required under that subsection, the Board shall provide the appropriate council with a further written statement giving any such particulars omitted from the earlier statement as soon as it is possible for them to do so.

**37.**—(1) This section applies where, immediately before the date on which any educational institution becomes an institution within the further education sector—

(a) it is maintained by a local education authority, or

(b) it is a designated assisted institution dependent on assistance from a local education authority,

1988 c. 40.

and in the financial year ending immediately before that date (referred to in this section as the "relevant financial year"), the institution was covered by a scheme under section 33 or 139 of the Education Reform Act 1988 (schemes for financing schools or institutions of further or higher education); and in this section, in relation to the institution, the scheme is referred to as the "applicable scheme" and the authority concerned as the "assisting authority".

(2) If the net expenditure of the institution for the relevant financial year is less than the net budget share of the institution for that year, the assisting authority shall pay to the new governing body of the institution a sum equal to the shortfall.

(3) If the net expenditure of the institution for the relevant financial year is greater than the net budget share of the institution for that year, the new governing body of the institution shall pay to the assisting authority a sum equal to the excess.

(4) In this section, in respect of any financial year of the institution—

"net budget share" means the budget share—

(i) less such amount as may be prescribed in respect of any earned income, and

(ii) plus such amount as may be prescribed in respect of any surplus, and

"net expenditure" means any expenditure, less such amount as may be prescribed in respect of earned income.

(5) Any sum payable under this section shall be paid in accordance with regulations, and the regulations may provide for sums to be payable by prescribed instalments and for sums to carry prescribed interest.

(6) Regulations may, in the case of any institution where the operative date falls within a financial year in which the institution was covered by such a scheme as is referred to in subsection (1) above, make provision for applying this section with modifications relating to the amounts that are to be taken for the purposes of this section to be the net budget share and the net expenditure of the institution for that year.

(7) In this section, in respect of any financial year of the institution—

"budget share" means the amount which is that institution's budget share for the relevant financial year for the purposes of Chapter III of Part I or Chapter III of Part II of the Education Reform Act 1988,

1988 c. 40.

"earned income" means any sums, other than sums appropriated for the purposes of the institution by the assisting authority, received by the institution in respect of the relevant financial year which the institution is authorised under the applicable scheme to retain, "expenditure" means such expenditure for the purposes of the institution incurred in the relevant financial year by the former governing body or the assisting authority as may be prescribed,

"financial year" has the same meaning as in the Education Reform Act 1988,

"former governing body" means the governing body of the institution immediately before the operative date and "new governing body" means the governing body of the institution on or after that date, and

"surplus" means the amount of any surplus which the institution is authorised under the applicable scheme to carry forward to the relevant financial year.

(8) In this section—

(a) references to a designated assisted institution are references to an institution designated by or under regulations made, or having effect as if made, under section 218(10)(b) of the Education Reform Act 1988 as an institution substantially dependent for its maintenance on assistance from local education authorities, and

(b) "prescribed" means prescribed by regulations.

(9) For the purposes of this section a designated assisted institution shall be regarded as dependent on assistance from a local education authority if it is assisted by that authority and either—

(a) it is not assisted by any other local education authority, or

(b) that authority provides a larger proportion than any other local education authority by whom the institution is assisted of the aggregate amount of the sums received by the governing body of the institution during any financial year by way of assistance from such authorities in respect of the expenses of maintaining the institution.

**38.**—(1) This section applies to any excepted loan liability, that is, any liability of a local authority which—

(a) in the case of a transfer by virtue of section 23 of this Act, would have been transferred but for subsection (3)(a) of that section,

(b) in the case of a transfer by virtue of section 32 of this Act, would have been transferred but for subsection (4)(a) of that section, or

(c) in the case of a transfer by virtue of section 34(4)(a) of this Act, could have been transferred but for subsection (5) of that section.

(2) A council may make payments, on such terms and conditions as the council may determine, to a local authority in respect of the principal of, and any interest on, any excepted loan liability of that authority.

(3) No payment shall be made under this section in respect of any excepted loan liability, where the class or classes of excepted loan liabilities in respect of which payments may be made are for the time being prescribed by an order of the Secretary of State, unless the liability falls within a prescribed class.

(4) The Secretary of State may by order provide for determining—

(a) the amounts that may be paid under this section in respect of the principal of, and any interest on, any excepted loan liability,

(b) the instalments by which any amounts may be paid, and

(c) the rate at which interest may be paid on any outstanding amounts,

and, in the case of any payment to which such an order applies, no amount may be paid under this section in excess of any amount determined in accordance with the order.

Control of disposals of land.

**39.**—(1) Subject to subsection (11) below, this section applies to any disposal during the controlled period—

(a) of land which, immediately before the beginning of that period, was used or held for the purposes of any relevant institution, or

(b) of land which was obtained before the beginning of that period for the purpose of being so used or held and had not before the beginning of that period been appropriated to any other use.

(2) For the purposes of this section and sections 41 and 43 of this Act, an institution is a relevant institution if—

(a) it is an educational institution maintained by a local education authority and falls within section 15(2) of this Act,

(b) it is a county school or controlled school and falls within section 15(3) of this Act, or

(c) it is an educational institution such as is mentioned in section 28(1) of this Act and meets the requirements of subsection (2)(a) or (b) of that section.

(3) In this section "the controlled period" means the period beginning with 22nd March 1991 and ending with—

(a) the operative date in relation to the institution in question or, if later, the date on which any matter relating to that land on which agreement is required to be reached under paragraph 2(1) of Schedule 5 to this Act is finally determined, or

(b) in the case of an institution falling within paragraph (c) above, 21st March 1995 if earlier.

(4) Except with the consent of the Secretary of State, no local authority shall after the passing of this Act make a disposal to which this section applies.

(5) If at any time after 21st March 1991 and before the passing of this Act such an authority have made a disposal which would have been in contravention of the provisions of subsection (4) above if they had then been in force the same consequences shall follow as if those provisions had been contravened by that authority.

(6) Any consent for the purposes of this section may be given either in respect of a particular disposal or in respect of disposals of any class or description and either unconditionally or subject to conditions.

(7) Any signification of consent for the purposes of this section, or of such consent subject to conditions, given by the Secretary of State before the passing of this Act in respect of any disposal to which this section applies, shall be treated for the purposes of this section as a consent, or a consent subject to the conditions, given under this section.

(8) This section has effect notwithstanding anything in section 123 of the Local Government Act 1972 (general power to dispose of land) or in any other enactment; and the consent required by this section shall be in addition to any consent required by subsection (2) of that section or by any other enactment.

(9) A disposal shall not be invalid or, in the case of a disposal which consists of a contract, void by reason only that it has been made or entered into in contravention of this section; and (subject to the provisions of section 40 of this Act) a person acquiring land, or entering into a contract to acquire land, from a local authority shall not be concerned to enquire whether any consent required by this section has been given or any conditions have been complied with.

(10) In this section references to disposing of land include—

    (a) granting or disposing of any interest in land,

    (b) entering into a contract to dispose of land or to grant or dispose of any such interest, and

    (c) granting an option to acquire any land or any such interest.

(11) This section does not apply to a disposal falling within subsection (10)(a) above if it is made in pursuance of a contract entered into, or an option granted, on or before 21st March 1991.

(12) Where at any time land is used for the purposes of an institution, any interest of a local authority in the land subsisting at that time shall be taken for the purposes of subsection (1) above to be land held for the purposes of that institution (whether or not it is by virtue of that interest that the land is so used).

**40.**—(1) This section applies where a local authority have made any disposal to which section 39 of this Act applies in contravention of that section (referred to below in this section as a wrongful disposal).

(2) Where a wrongful disposal consists in entering into a contract to dispose of any land or to grant or dispose of any interest in land, the Education Assets Board may by notice in writing served on the other party to the contract repudiate the contract at any time before the conveyance or grant of the land or interest in land to which it relates is completed or executed.

(3) Where a wrongful disposal consists in granting an option to acquire any land or any interest in land, the Education Assets Board may by notice in writing served on the option holder repudiate the option at any time before it is exercised.

(4) A repudiation under subsection (2) or (3) above shall have effect as if made by the local authority concerned.

(5) Where a wrongful disposal consists in granting or disposing of any interest in land (whether or not in pursuance of any earlier disposal of a description falling within subsection (2) or (3) above) the Education Assets Board may be authorised by the Secretary of State to purchase compulsorily the interest in land which was the subject of the disposal.

1981 c. 67.

(6) The Acquisition of Land Act 1981 shall apply in relation to the compulsory purchase of land under subsection (5) above as if references in sections 12 and 13 of that Act to every owner of the land included references to the local authority concerned.

(7) On completion of a compulsory purchase under that subsection of any interest in land, the Education Assets Board shall convey that interest to the appropriate transferee.

(8) In subsection (7) above, "the appropriate transferee" means—

(a) where the interest disposed of, or the land in which the interest was granted, was—

(i) used or held by the local authority concerned for the purposes of an institution to which section 39(2)(a) or (b) of this Act applies, or

(ii) obtained by that authority for the purpose of being so used or held,

the further education corporation established under this Act to conduct that institution, and

(b) where the interest disposed of, or the land in which the interest was granted, was—

(i) so used or held for the purposes of an institution to which section 39(2)(c) of this Act applies, or

(ii) obtained by the authority concerned for the purpose of being so used or held,

the appropriate transferee within the meaning of section 32 of this Act in relation to that institution.

(9) Where the Education Assets Board acquire any interest in land by a compulsory purchase under subsection (5) above the Board shall be entitled to recover from the local authority concerned an amount equal to the aggregate of—

(a) the amount of compensation agreed or awarded in respect of that purchase, together with any interest payable by the Board in respect of that compensation in accordance with section 11 of the Compulsory Purchase Act 1965 or section 52A of the Land Compensation Act 1973, and

1965 c. 56.
1973 c. 26.

(b) the amount of the costs and expenses incurred by the Board in connection with the making of the compulsory purchase order.

Control of contracts.

**41.**—(1) This section applies, subject to subsection (5) below, to any contract which, if a relevant institution were to become an institution within the further education sector, would or might on or after the operative date bind the governing body of the institution.

(2) Except with the appropriate consent, a local authority shall not after the passing of this Act enter into a contract to which this section applies.

(3) If at any time after 21st March 1991 and before the passing of this Act a local authority have entered into a contract which would have been in contravention of the provisions of subsection (2) above if they had then been in force, the same consequences shall follow as if those provisions had been contravened by the local authority.

(4) In relation to any contract the appropriate consent is—

(a) the consent of the existing governing body of the institution, and

(b) if (on the assumption in subsection (1) above) the contract will require the governing body of the institution to make payments on or after 1st April 1993 amounting in aggregate to £50,000 or more, the consent of the Secretary of State.

(5) This section does not apply to—

(a) a works contract (within the meaning of Part III of the Local Government, Planning and Land Act 1980) which is entered into in accordance with section 7 of that Act, or

(b) a works contract (within the meaning of Part I of the Local Government Act 1988) which is entered into in accordance with section 4 of that Act.

1980 c. 65.

1988 c. 9.

(6) Any consent for the purposes of this section may be given either in respect of a particular contract or in respect of contracts of any class or description and either unconditionally or subject to conditions.

(7) Any signification of consent for the purposes of this section, or of such consent subject to conditions, given by the governing body of an institution or the Secretary of State before the passing of this Act in respect of any contract to which this section applies shall be treated for the purposes of this section as a consent, or a consent subject to the conditions, given under this section.

(8) A contract shall not be void by reason only that it has been entered into in contravention of this section and (subject to section 42 of this Act) a person entering into a contract with a local authority shall not be concerned to enquire whether any consent required by this section has been given or any conditions of such a consent have been complied with.

(9) Where there is an obligation under a contract to which this section applies to provide any benefit other than money, subsection (4)(b) above shall apply as if the obligation were to pay a sum of money corresponding to the value of the benefit to the recipient.

(10) This section does not apply to a contract to dispose of land or to grant or dispose of any interest in land.

**42.**—(1) This section applies where a local authority have entered into a contract to which section 41 of this Act applies in contravention of that section.

Wrongful contracts.

(2) The Education Assets Board may by notice in writing served on the other party to the contract repudiate the contract at any time before it is performed.

(3) A repudiation under subsection (2) above shall have effect as if made by the local authority concerned.

**43.**—(1) Where, in consequence of a determination by the local education authority or any other person of the rate of remuneration of any employees, the rate of remuneration of any relevant employees would, apart from this section, be increased as from a date (referred to in this section as the "proposed date of increase") falling after 1st September 1992, the authority—

   (a) shall notify the Secretary of State in writing of the determination and the proposed date of increase, and

   (b) shall not pay any relevant employee at the new rate unless the increase is authorised under this section by the Secretary of State.

(2) In this section "relevant employees" means persons who are employed at institutions which are relevant institutions by virtue of section 39(2)(a) or (b) of this Act.

(3) This section does not apply to remuneration determined in accordance with the scales and other provisions set out or referred to in a pay and conditions order (within the meaning of the School Teachers' Pay and Conditions Act 1991).

(4) Where the Secretary of State receives a notification under subsection (1) above, he shall, before the end of the period of four weeks beginning with the day on which he received the notification, either—

   (a) authorise the increase resulting from the determination so far as it relates to relevant employees, or

   (b) afford to the authority, and to such persons appearing to him to be representative of relevant employees affected by the determination as he considers appropriate, an opportunity of making representations to him in respect of the determination.

(5) After considering any representations made to him under subsection (4)(b) above, the Secretary of State shall—

   (a) authorise the increase resulting from the determination, or

   (b) refuse to authorise the increase,

so far as it relates to relevant employees.

(6) The Secretary of State shall give written notification of any decision under subsection (4)(a) or (5) above to the local education authority and, in the case of subsection (5) above, to any other persons who made representations to him under subsection (4)(b) above.

(7) Subsection (8) below applies where—

   (a) by virtue of this section a relevant employee is not paid at the new rate on the proposed date of increase, but

   (b) the Secretary of State authorises the increase after that date.

(8) Where this subsection applies, the employee concerned shall, for the purpose of determining the terms of any contract affected by section 26 of this Act, be regarded as having been entitled under his contract of employment to be paid by the local education authority at the new rate as from the proposed date of increase.

*Miscellaneous*

**44.**—(1) In this section "institution of voluntary origin" means a further education institution which, when it became a further education institution, was a voluntary school or a grant-maintained school which was a voluntary school before it became grant-maintained.

(2) The governing body of every further education institution except an institution which on the appointed day was a college of further education shall ensure that at an appropriate time on at least one day in each week during which the institution is open an act of collective worship is held at the institution which persons receiving education at the institution may attend.

(3) In an institution of voluntary origin such act of collective worship shall —

    (a) be in such forms as to comply with the provisions of any trust deed affecting the institution, and

    (b) reflect the religious traditions and practices of the institution before it became a further education institution.

(4) In all other further education institutions such act of collective worship shall be wholly or mainly of a broadly Christian character in that it shall reflect the broad traditions of Christian belief but need not be distinctive of any particular Christian denomination.

(5) If the governing body of a further education institution considers it appropriate to do so it may in addition to the act of collective worship referred to in subsection (3) or (4) provide for acts of worship which reflect the practices of some or all of the other religious traditions represented in Great Britain.

(6) In this section "the appointed day" means the day appointed under section 94 of this Act for the commencement of subsection (4) of section 15 of this Act.

**45.**—(1) In this section "institution of voluntary origin" means a further education institution which, when it became a further education institution, was a voluntary school or a grant-maintained school which was a voluntary school before it became grant-maintained.

(2) The governing body of every further education institution except an institution which on the appointed day was a college of further education shall ensure that religious education is provided at the institution for all persons attending the institution who wish to receive it.

(3) The governing body of a further education institution shall be deemed to be fulfilling its duty under this section if religious education is provided at a time or times at which it is convenient for the majority of full time students to attend.

(4) For the purposes of this section religious education may take the form of a course of lectures or classes or of single lectures or classes provided on a regular basis and may include a course of study leading to an examination or the award of a qualification.

(5) The form and content of religious education provided pursuant to this section shall be determined from time to time by the governing body of each further education institution and—

    (a) in the case of an institution of voluntary origin—

(i) shall be in accordance with the provisions of any trust deed affecting the institution, and

(ii) shall not be contrary to the religious traditions of the institution before it became a further education institution;

(b) in the case of all further education institutions shall reflect the fact that the religious traditions in Great Britain are in the main Christian whilst taking account of the teaching and practices of the other principal religions represented in Great Britain.

(6) In this section "the appointed day" means the day appointed under section 94 of this Act for the commencement of subsection (4) of section 15 of this Act.

Variation of trust deeds.

**46.**—(1) The Secretary of State may by order make such modifications as he thinks fit in any trust deed or other instrument—

(a) relating to or regulating an institution within the further education sector, or

(b) relating to any land or other property held by any person for the purposes of such an institution.

(2) Before making any modifications under subsection (1) above of any trust deed or other instrument the Secretary of State shall so far as it appears to him to be practicable to do so consult—

(a) the governing body of the institution,

(b) where that deed or instrument, or any other instrument relating to or regulating the institution concerned, confers power on any other persons to modify or replace that deed or instrument, those persons, and

(c) where the instrument to be modified is a trust deed and the trustees are different from the persons mentioned in paragraphs (a) and (b) above, the trustees.

Transfer of higher education institutions to further education sector.

**47.**—(1) The Secretary of State may by order provide for the transfer of a higher education corporation to the further education sector.

(2) Where an order is made under this section in respect of a higher education corporation, sections 20 and 21 of this Act shall have effect as if, on the date the order has effect, the corporation were established as a further education corporation; and the order may make any provision that may be made by an order under section 15 of this Act specifying a grant-maintained school.

(3) On such date as may be specified in the order the corporation shall cease to be a higher education corporation and become a further education corporation.

(4) An order under section 28 of this Act in respect of any institution may revoke any order in respect of that institution under section 129 of the Education Reform Act 1988 (designation of institutions).

1988 c. 40.

Statutory conditions of employment.

**48.**—(1) This section applies where—

(a) an educational institution at which a school teacher is employed by a local education authority, or by the governing body of a voluntary or grant-maintained school, becomes an institution within the further education sector, and

(b) immediately before the operative date, any of the terms and conditions of his employment have effect by virtue of a pay and conditions order.

(2) As from the operative date the person's contract of employment shall have effect—

   (a) in relation to him and to the governing body of the institution as it had effect immediately before that date in relation to school teachers and to local education authorities or governing bodies of voluntary or grant-maintained schools, and

   (b) as if the contract required any remuneration determined in accordance with the scales and other provisions set out or referred to in the relevant pay and conditions order to be paid to him by the governing body of the institution.

(3) Nothing in this section affects any right to vary the terms of any contract of employment.

(4) In this section—

   (a) "pay and conditions order" and "school teacher" have the same meaning as in the School Teachers' Pay and Conditions Act 1991, and

   (b) "relevant pay and conditions order", in relation to any person, means the pay and conditions order having effect in relation to him immediately before the operative date or, if that order is no longer in force, the pay and conditions order which would have had effect in relation to him if the institution at which he is employed had not become an institution within the further education sector.

**49.**—(1) This section applies to any contract made between the governing body of an institution within the further education sector and any person employed by them, not being a contract made in contemplation of the employee's pending dismissal by reason of redundancy.

(2) In so far as a contract to which this section applies provides that the employee—

   (a) shall not be dismissed by reason of redundancy, or

   (b) if he is so dismissed, shall be paid a sum in excess of the sum which the employer is liable to pay to him under section 81 of the Employment Protection (Consolidation) Act 1978,

the contract shall be void and of no effect.

**50.**—(1) The Secretary of State may by regulations require the governing body of any institution within the further education sector to publish such information as may be prescribed about—

   (a) the educational provision made or proposed to be made for their students,

   (b) the educational achievements of their students on entry to the institution and the educational achievements of their students while at the institution (including in each case the results of examinations, tests and other assessments),

(c) the financial and other resources of the institution and the effectiveness of the use made of such resources, and

(d) the careers of their students after completing any course or leaving the institution.

(2) For the purposes of subsection (1)(d) above, a person's career includes any education, training, employment or occupation; and the regulations may in particular require the published information to show—

(a) the numbers of students not undertaking any career, and

(b) the persons providing students with education, training or employment.

(3) The information shall be published in such form and manner and at such times as may be prescribed.

(4) The published information shall not name any student to whom it relates.

(5) In this section "prescribed" means prescribed by regulations.

Publication of proposals.

**51.**—(1) A council shall not make a proposal for—

(a) the establishment by the Secretary of State of a body corporate under section 16(1) of this Act,

(b) the establishment by the Secretary of State of a body corporate under subsection (3) of that section, or

(c) the dissolution of any further education corporation by the Secretary of State under section 27 of this Act,

unless the following conditions have been complied with.

(2) The conditions are that—

(a) a draft of the proposal, or of a proposal in substantially the same form, giving such information as may be prescribed has been published by such time and in such manner as may be prescribed,

(b) the council have considered any representations about the draft made to them within the prescribed period, and

(c) copies of the draft and of any such representations have been sent to the Secretary of State.

(3) The Secretary of State shall not make—

(a) an order under section 16(1) of this Act, other than an order made for the purpose of giving effect to a proposal by a council, or

(b) an order under section 16(2) of this Act,

unless he has published a draft of the proposed order, or of an order in substantially the same form, by such time and in such manner as may be prescribed.

(4) In this section "prescribed" means prescribed by regulations.

**52.**—(1) This section applies where an institution within the further education sector provides full-time education suitable to the requirements of persons over compulsory school age who have not attained the age of nineteen years.

(2) A council may by notice given to the governing body of such an institution—

(a) require them to provide for such individuals as may be specified in the notice such education falling within subsection (1) above as is appropriate to their abilities and aptitudes, or

(b) withdraw such a requirement.

(3) The governing body of such an institution shall, for any academic year in respect of which they receive financial support from a council, secure compliance with any requirement in respect of any individual who has not attained the age of nineteen years which is or has been imposed by that council under subsection (2) above and has not been withdrawn.

**53.**—(1) The accounts of—

(a) any further education corporation, and

(b) any designated institution,

shall be open to the inspection of the Comptroller and Auditor General.

(2) In the case of any such corporation or institution—

(a) the power conferred by subsection (1) above, and

(b) the powers under sections 6 and 8 of the National Audit Act 1983 (examinations into the economy, efficiency and effectiveness of certain bodies and access to documents and information) conferred on the Comptroller and Auditor General by virtue of section 6(3)(c) of that Act,

shall be exercisable only in, or in relation to accounts or other documents which relate to, any financial year in which expenditure is incurred by the corporation, or by the governing body of the institution in question, in respect of which grants, loans or other payments are made to them under this Part of this Act.

CHAPTER III

GENERAL

**54.**—(1) Each of the following shall give a council such information as they may require for the purposes of the exercise of any of their functions under this Part of this Act—

(a) a local education authority,

(b) the governing body of any institution maintained by a local education authority, grant-maintained school, city technology college or city college for the technology of the arts,

(c) the governing body of any institution within the further education sector or the higher education sector, and

(d) the governing body of any institution which is receiving or has received financial support under section 5 of this Act.

(2) Such information relating to the provision which has been made by a local education authority in respect of any pupil at an institution as the authority may require for the purposes of claiming any amount in respect of the pupil from another authority under section 51 of the Education (No. 2) Act 1986 or by virtue of regulations under section 52 of that Act shall, where the institution becomes an institution within the further education sector, be provided to the authority by the governing body of the institution.

Inspection etc. of local education authority institutions, other than schools, and advice to Secretary of State.

**55.**—(1) The chief inspector shall have the general duty of keeping the Secretary of State informed about—

(a) the quality of education provided in local education authority institutions,

(b) the educational standards achieved in such institutions, and

(c) whether the financial resources made available to such institutions are managed efficiently.

(2) When asked to do so by the Secretary of State, the chief inspector shall—

(a) give advice to the Secretary of State on such matters relating to local education authority institutions, and on such other matters relating to further education, as may be specified in the Secretary of State's request, and

(b) inspect and report on any such local education authority institution, or any such class of local education authority institution, as may be so specified.

(3) In connection with the duties imposed on the chief inspector under this section, his powers, and those of his inspectors, in relation to the inspection of schools under any enactment shall extend to the inspection of institutions under this section.

(4) In relation to any local education authority institution maintained or assisted by them, a local education authority—

(a) shall keep under review the quality of education provided, the educational standards achieved and whether the financial resources made available are managed efficiently, and

(b) may cause an inspection to be made by persons authorised by them.

(5) A local education authority shall not authorise any person to inspect any institution under this section unless they are satisfied that he is suitably qualified to do so.

(6) A person who wilfully obstructs any person authorised to inspect an institution under or by virtue of this section in the exercise of his functions shall be guilty of an offence and liable on summary conviction to a fine not exceeding level 4 on the standard scale.

(7) In this section—

(a) in relation to institutions in England, "chief inspector" means Her Majesty's Chief Inspector of Schools in England and "his inspectors" means Her Majesty's Inspectors of Schools in England,

(b) in relation to institutions in Wales, "chief inspector" means Her Majesty's Chief Inspector of Schools in Wales and "his inspectors" means Her Majesty's Inspectors of Schools in Wales, and

(c) "local education authority institution" means an educational institution, other than a school, maintained or assisted by a local education authority.

**56.**—(1) In exercising their functions under this Part of this Act, each council shall comply with any directions contained in an order made by the Secretary of State.

(2) Directions under this section may be general or special, and special directions may, in particular, relate to the provision of financial support by the council in respect of activities carried on by any particular institution or institutions.

Directions.

**57.**—(1) If the Secretary of State is satisfied that the affairs of any institution within the further education sector have been or are being mismanaged, he may on the recommendation of the appropriate council by order—

(a) remove all or any of the members of the governing body of the institution and appoint new members in their places, and

(b) make such modifications of the instrument of government of the institution as he thinks fit.

Intervention in the event of mismanagement or breach of duty.

(2) An appointment of a member of a governing body of an institution under subsection (1) above shall have effect as if made in accordance with the instrument of government and articles of government of the institution.

(3) If the Secretary of State is satisfied, either upon complaint by any person interested or otherwise, that—

(a) a council, or

(b) the governing body of any institution within the further education sector,

have failed to discharge any duty imposed on them by or for the purposes of the Education Acts, he may make an order under this subsection.

(4) An order under subsection (3) above shall declare the council or the governing body, as the case may be, to be in default in respect of that duty, and may give such directions for the purpose of enforcing the execution of that duty as appear to the Secretary of State to be expedient.

(5) A council or governing body in respect of which an order is made under subsection (3) above shall comply with any directions contained in the order.

(6) Section 93 of the Education Act 1944 (power to hold local inquiries) applies for the purposes of the Secretary of State's functions under this section as it applies for the purposes of his functions under that Act.

1944 c. 31.

PART I
Reorganisations of
schools involving
establishment of
further education
corporation.

**58.**—(1) Subsection (2) below applies where, in connection with a reorganisation of schools maintained by a local education authority, any land used for the purposes of one or more of the schools affected by the reorganisation or, as the case may be, the school so affected—

(a) is to cease to be so used or is to continue to be so used for a limited period, and

(b) while it is so used, or after it has ceased to be so used, is to be used for the purposes of an institution conducted by a further education corporation;

and in that subsection that land is referred to as "the land to be transferred".

(2) If the land to be transferred is land of the local authority, the land and any other property of the local authority used for the purposes of the school on that land shall be treated for the purposes of section 23 of this Act as used for the purposes of the educational institution conducted by the corporation.

(3) For the purposes of this section there is a reorganisation of schools maintained by a local education authority if, in the case of each of the schools affected by the reorganisation or (if there is only one) the school so affected—

(a) the local education authority cease to maintain the school, or

(b) a significant change is made in the character of the school or the premises of the school are significantly enlarged,

whether or not the reorganisation also involves the establishment of one or more new schools.

**59.**—(1) This subsection applies where—

(a) the governors of a school maintained by a local education authority as a voluntary school intend to discontinue the school, and

(b) the intention arises in connection with a proposal by a council, or by the Secretary of State, for the establishment under section 16 of this Act of a further education corporation to conduct an educational institution in the same area.

(2) Where subsection (1) above applies—

(a) section 14 of the Education Act 1944 (restrictions on discontinuance) shall not apply,

(b) section 13 of the Education Act 1980 (establishment and alteration of voluntary schools) and, so far as relating to that section, section 16(1) to (3B) of that Act, shall apply as they would apply if the intention were to make a significant change in the character of the school, and

(c) if the school is discontinued the duty of the local education authority to maintain the school as a voluntary school shall be extinguished.

(3) Where—

(a) a local education authority intend to cease to maintain any county school or (except as provided by section 14 of the Education Act 1944) voluntary school or to make any significant change in the character of a county school, or

(b) the governors of a school maintained by a local education authority as a voluntary school intend to discontinue the school or to make any significant change in the character of the school,

and ceasing to maintain or discontinuing the school, or the change, will affect the facilities for full-time education suitable to the requirements of persons over compulsory school age who have not attained the age of nineteen years, they shall, before they publish notice of their proposals in pursuance of section 12 or 13 of the Education Act 1980 or serve notice under section 14 of the Education Act 1944, consult the appropriate council.

1980 c. 20.
1944 c. 31.

(4) In subsection (3) above, references to any significant change in the character of a school include a significant enlargement of its premises.

(5) Where—

(a) a local education authority propose to make any change in any arrangements for any special school as to the pupils for whom provision is made or the special educational provision made for them or propose to cease to maintain any special school, and

(b) the change, or ceasing to maintain the school, will affect the facilities for full-time education suitable to the requirements of persons over compulsory school age who have not attained the age of nineteen years,

they shall, before they give written notice of the proposed change to the Secretary of State in pursuance of regulations under section 12 of the Education Act 1981 (approval of special schools) or serve notice of their proposals under section 14 of that Act (discontinuance of maintained special school), consult the appropriate council.

1981 c. 60.

**60.** No function conferred or imposed by this Act on a further education funding council shall be construed as relating to any person who is detained, otherwise than at a school, in pursuance of an order made by a court or of an order of recall made by the Secretary of State.

Saving as to persons detained by order of a court.

**61.**—(1) In this Part of this Act—

Interpretation of Part I.

"functions" includes powers and duties,

"modifications" includes additions, alterations and omissions and "modify" shall be construed accordingly, and

"regulations" means regulations made by the Secretary of State.

(2) References in this Part of this Act, except section 26, to the transfer of any person's rights or liabilities do not include—

(a) rights or liabilities under a contract of employment, or

(b) liabilities of that person in respect of compensation for premature retirement of any person formerly employed by him.

(3) In relation to any time before the commencement of section 65 of this Act, references in this Part of this Act and, so far as relating to this Part, Part III of this Act—

(a) to institutions within the higher education sector are to universities, to institutions within the PCFC funding sector and to higher education institutions which receive, or are maintained by persons who receive, grants under regulations made under section 100(1)(b) of the Education Act 1944, and

(b) to a higher education funding council are to the Universities Funding Council established under section 131 of the Education Reform Act 1988 and to the Polytechnics and Colleges Funding Council established under section 132 of that Act.

## PART II

### HIGHER EDUCATION

#### *The new funding councils*

The Higher Education Funding Councils.

**62.**—(1) There shall be established—

(a) a body corporate to be known as the Higher Education Funding Council for England to exercise in relation to England the functions conferred on them, and

(b) a body corporate to be known as the Higher Education Funding Council for Wales to exercise in relation to Wales the functions conferred on them.

(2) The Higher Education Funding Council for England shall consist of not less than twelve nor more than fifteen members appointed by the Secretary of State, of whom one shall be so appointed as chairman.

(3) The Higher Education Funding Council for Wales shall consist of not less than eight nor more than twelve members appointed by the Secretary of State, of whom one shall be so appointed as chairman.

(4) In appointing the members of a council the Secretary of State—

(a) shall have regard to the desirability of including persons who appear to him to have experience of, and to have shown capacity in, the provision of higher education or to have held, and to have shown capacity in, any position carrying responsibility for the provision of higher education and, in appointing such persons, he shall have regard to the desirability of their being currently engaged in the provision of higher education or in carrying responsibility for such provision, and

(b) shall have regard to the desirability of including persons who appear to him to have experience of, and to have shown capacity in, industrial, commercial or financial matters or the practice of any profession.

(5) In this Part of this Act any reference to a council is to a higher education funding council.

(6) In the Education Acts any reference to a higher education funding council—

(a) in relation to matters falling within the responsibility of the Higher Education Funding Council for England or to educational institutions in England, is to that council, and

(b) in relation to matters falling within the responsibility of the Higher Education Funding Council for Wales or to educational institutions in Wales, is to that council.

(7) In this Part of this Act references to institutions in England or institutions in Wales—

    (a) are to institutions whose activities are carried on, or principally carried on, in England or, as the case may be, Wales, but

    (b) include, in both cases, the Open University.

(8) Any dispute as to whether any functions are exercisable by one of the councils shall be determined by the Secretary of State.

(9) Schedule 1 to this Act has effect with respect to each of the councils.

**63.**—(1) On the appointed day—

    (a) the Universities Funding Council and the Polytechnics and Colleges Funding Council (referred to in this section as the "existing councils") shall be dissolved, and

    (b) all property, rights and liabilities to which either of the existing councils were entitled or subject immediately before that date shall become by virtue of this section property, rights and liabilities of the Higher Education Funding Council for England,

but this subsection does not apply to rights or liabilities under a contract of employment.

Dissolution of existing councils.

(2) Where—

    (a) immediately before the appointed day, a person (referred to below as "the employee") is employed by an existing council (referred to below as "the existing employer") under a contract of employment which would have continued but for the dissolution of the existing employer, and

    (b) the employee is designated for the purposes of this section by an order made by the Secretary of State,

the contract of employment shall not be terminated by that dissolution but shall have effect as from the appointed day as if originally made between the employee and the new employer.

(3) In this section "the new employer", in relation to the employee, means such higher education funding council as may be specified in relation to the employee by the order designating him for the purposes of this section; and in this subsection "higher education funding council" includes the Scottish Higher Education Funding Council.

(4) Without prejudice to subsection (2) above, where that subsection applies—

    (a) all the existing employer's rights, powers, duties and liabilities under or in connection with the contract of employment shall by virtue of this section be transferred on the appointed day to the new employer, and

    (b) anything done before that date by or in relation to the existing employer in respect of that contract or the employee shall as from that date be treated as having been done by or in relation to the new employer.

PART II

(5) Subsections (2) and (4) above are without prejudice to any right of the employee to terminate his contract of employment if a substantial change is made to his detriment in his working conditions, but no such right shall arise by reason only of the change in employer effected by this section.

(6) An order under this section may designate a person either individually or as a member of a class or description of employees.

(7) In this section "the appointed day" means the day appointed under section 94 of this Act for the commencement of this section.

Transitional
arrangements.

1988 c. 40.

64.—(1) Until the commencement of section 65 of this Act, any institution which is a university and was at any time within the PCFC funding sector shall be treated for the purposes of Chapter II of Part II of the Education Reform Act 1988 (reorganisation and provision of funding of higher education) as if it were within that sector and were not a university.

(2) Until their dissolution the Universities Funding Council shall give to the higher education funding councils and the Scottish Higher Education Funding Council all such assistance as those councils may reasonably require for the purpose of enabling them to exercise their functions on and after the commencement of section 65 of this Act or, as the case may be, the corresponding provisions of the Further and Higher Education (Scotland) Act 1992.

1992 c. 37.

(3) Until their dissolution the Polytechnics and Colleges Funding Council shall give to the higher education funding councils all such assistance as those councils may reasonably require for the purpose of enabling them to exercise their functions on and after the commencement of section 65 of this Act.

(4) The Higher Education Funding Council for England shall discharge any duty under paragraph 17 of Schedule 8 to the Education Reform Act 1988 (accounts) in respect of any period ending before the dissolution of the Universities Funding Council and the Polytechnics and Colleges Funding Council under section 63 of this Act which would have fallen to be discharged by those councils after the dissolution or fell to be so discharged before the dissolution but has not been discharged.

*Funds*

Administration of
funds by councils.

65.—(1) Each council shall be responsible, subject to the provisions of this Part of this Act, for administering funds made available to the council by the Secretary of State and others for the purposes of providing financial support for activities eligible for funding under this section.

(2) The activities eligible for funding under this section are—

(a) the provision of education and the undertaking of research by higher education institutions in the council's area,

(b) the provision of any facilities, and the carrying on of any other activities, by higher education institutions in their area which the governing bodies of those institutions consider it necessary or desirable to provide or carry on for the purpose of or in connection with education or research,

(c) the provision—

   (i) by institutions in their area maintained or assisted by local education authorities, or

   (ii) by such institutions in their area as are within the further education sector,

  of prescribed courses of higher education, and

 (d) the provision by any person of services for the purposes of, or in connection with, the provision of education or the undertaking of research by institutions within the higher education sector.

(3) A council may—

 (a) make grants, loans or other payments to the governing body of any higher education institution in respect of expenditure incurred or to be incurred by them for the purposes of any activities eligible for funding under this section by virtue of subsection (2)(a) or (b) above, and

 (b) make grants, loans or other payments to any persons in respect of expenditure incurred or to be incurred by them for the purposes of the provision as mentioned in subsection (2)(c) above of prescribed courses of higher education or the provision of services as mentioned in subsection (2)(d) above,

subject in each case to such terms and conditions as the council think fit.

(4) The terms and conditions on which a council may make any grants, loans or other payments under this section may in particular—

 (a) enable the council to require the repayment, in whole or in part, of sums paid by the council if any of the terms and conditions subject to which the sums were paid is not complied with, and

 (b) require the payment of interest in respect of any period during which a sum due to the council in accordance with any of the terms and conditions remains unpaid,

but shall not relate to the application by the body to whom the grants or other payments are made of any sums derived otherwise than from the council.

(5) In this section and section 66 of this Act "higher education institution" means a university, an institution conducted by a higher education corporation or a designated institution.

**66.**—(1) Before exercising their discretion under section 65(3)(a) of this Act with respect to the terms and conditions to be imposed in relation to any grants, loans or other payments, a council shall consult such of the following bodies as appear to the council to be appropriate to consult in the circumstances—

 (a) such bodies representing the interests of higher education institutions as appear to the council to be concerned, and

 (b) the governing body of any particular higher education institution which appears to the council to be concerned.

(2) In exercising their functions in relation to the provision of financial support for activities eligible for funding under section 65 of this Act a council shall have regard to the desirability of not discouraging any institution for whose activities financial support is provided under that section from maintaining or developing its funding from other sources.

*Administration of funds: supplementary.*

PART II

(3) In exercising those functions a council shall have regard (so far as they think it appropriate to do so in the light of any other relevant considerations) to the desirability of maintaining—

(a) what appears to them to be an appropriate balance in the support given by them as between institutions which are of a denominational character and other institutions, and

(b) any distinctive characteristics of any institution within the higher education sector for whose activities financial support is provided under that section.

(4) For the purposes of subsection (3) above an institution is an institution of a denominational character if it appears to the council that either—

(a) at least one quarter of the members of the governing body of the institution are persons appointed to represent the interests of a religion or religious denomination,

(b) any of the property held for the purposes of the institution is held upon trusts which provide that, in the event of the discontinuance of the institution, the property concerned shall be held for, or sold and the proceeds of sale applied for, the benefit of a religion or religious denomination, or

(c) any of the property held for the purposes of the institution is held on trust for or in connection with—

(i) the provision of education, or

(ii) the conduct of an educational institution,

in accordance with the tenets of a religion or religious denomination.

Payments in respect of persons employed in provision of higher or further education.
1988 c. 40.

67.—(1) In section 133 of the Education Reform Act 1988 (payments by PCFC in respect of persons employed in the provision of higher or further education) for subsection (1) there is substituted—

"(1) A higher education funding council shall have power to make payments, subject to such terms and conditions as the council think fit, to—

(a) any local education authority in their area;

(b) the London Residuary Body;

(c) the London Pensions Fund Authority; and

(d) the governing body of any institution designated under section 129 of this Act, as originally enacted;

in respect of relevant expenditure incurred or to be incurred by that authority or body of any class or description prescribed for the purposes of this section."

(2) In subsection (2)(a) of that section (meaning of relevant expenditure) after "education authority" there is inserted "the London Residuary Body or the London Pensions Fund Authority".

(3) At the end of subsection (3) of that section (meaning of references to higher and further education) there is added "and in any other case the reference to further education shall be read as a reference to further education within the meaning of section 41 of the 1944 Act as that section had effect on that date".

(4) In subsection (4) of that section (duty to give information) after paragraph (a) there is inserted—

> "(aa) the London Residuary Body;
>
> (ab) the London Pensions Fund Authority".

(5) That section as originally enacted shall have effect, or be treated as having had effect, as if—

>  (a) in subsection (1), in relation to anything done before regulations for the purposes of that subsection were in force, the words "of any class or description prescribed for the purposes of this section" were omitted, and
>
>  (b) in subsections (1) and (2) the references to a local education authority included the London Residuary Body and the London Pensions Fund Authority.

**68.**—(1) The Secretary of State may make grants to each of the councils of such amounts and subject to such terms and conditions as he may determine.

(2) The terms and conditions subject to which grants are made by the Secretary of State to either of the councils—

>  (a) may in particular impose requirements to be complied with in respect of every institution, or every institution falling within a class or description specified in the terms and conditions, being requirements to be complied with in the case of any institution to which the requirements apply before financial support of any amount or description so specified is provided by the council in respect of activities carried on by the institution, but
>
>  (b) shall not otherwise relate to the provision of financial support by the council in respect of activities carried on by any particular institution or institutions.

(3) Such terms and conditions may not be framed by reference to particular courses of study or programmes of research (including the contents of such courses or programmes and the manner in which they are taught, supervised or assessed) or to the criteria for the selection and appointment of academic staff and for the admission of students.

(4) Such terms and conditions may in particular—

>  (a) enable the Secretary of State to require the repayment, in whole or in part, of sums paid by him if any of the terms and conditions subject to which the sums were paid is not complied with, and
>
>  (b) require the payment of interest in respect of any period during which a sum due to the Secretary of State in accordance with any of the terms and conditions remains unpaid.

### *Further functions*

**69.**—(1) Each council—

>  (a) shall provide the Secretary of State with such information or advice relating to the provision for their area of higher education as he may from time to time require, and

(b) may provide the Secretary of State with such information or advice relating to such provision as they think fit,

and information and advice provided under this subsection shall be provided in such manner as the Secretary of State may from time to time determine.

(2) Each council shall keep under review activities eligible for funding under section 65 of this Act.

(3) A council may provide, on such terms as may be agreed, such advisory services as the Department of Education for Northern Ireland or the Department of Agriculture for Northern Ireland may require in connection with the discharge of the department's functions relating to higher education in Northern Ireland.

(4) Where—

(a) any land or other property is or was used or held for the purposes of an institution, and

(b) the Secretary of State is entitled to any right or interest in respect of the property, or would be so entitled on the occurrence of any event,

then, if the institution is within the higher education sector, the Secretary of State may direct that all or any of his functions in respect of the property shall be exercisable on his behalf by the council, and the functions shall be so exercised in accordance with such directions as he may give from time to time.

(5) The Secretary of State may by order confer or impose on a council such supplementary functions relating to the provision of education as he thinks fit.

(6) For the purposes of subsection (5) above a function is a supplementary function in relation to a council if it is exercisable for the purposes of—

(a) the exercise by the Secretary of State of functions of his under any enactment, or

(b) the doing by the Secretary of State of anything he has power to do apart from any enactment,

and it relates to, or to the activities of, any institution mentioned in subsection (7) below.

(7) Those institutions are—

(a) institutions within the higher education sector, or

(b) institutions within the further education sector, or maintained or assisted by local education authorities, at which prescribed courses of higher education are currently provided.

Assessment of quality of education provided by institutions.

**70.**—(1) Each council shall—

(a) secure that provision is made for assessing the quality of education provided in institutions for whose activities they provide, or are considering providing, financial support under this Part of this Act, and

(b) establish a committee, to be known as the "Quality Assessment Committee", with the function of giving them advice on the discharge of their duty under paragraph (a) above and such other functions as may be conferred on the committee by the council.

(2) The majority of the members of the committee—

(a) shall be persons falling within subsection (3) below, and

(b) shall not be members of the council.

(3) Persons fall within this subsection if they appear to the council to have experience of, and to have shown capacity in, the provision of higher education in institutions within the higher education sector and, in appointing such persons, the council shall have regard to the desirability of their being currently engaged in the provision of higher education or in carrying responsibility for such provision.

(4) Schedule 1 to this Act shall apply to a committee established under this section as it applies to committees established under paragraph 8 of that Schedule.

*Institutions in the higher education sector*

**71.**—(1) After section 124 of the Education Reform Act 1988 there is inserted—

Higher education corporations: constitution and conduct. 1988 c. 40.

"Constitution and conduct of corporations.

124A.—(1) For each higher education corporation established on or after the appointed day there shall be an instrument (to be known as the instrument of government) providing for the constitution of the corporation and making such other provision as is required under this section.

(2) The initial instrument of government of a higher education corporation established on or after that day shall be such as is prescribed by an order of the Privy Council.

(3) An order of the Privy Council may—

(a) make an instrument of government of any higher education corporation with respect to which Schedule 7 to this Act has effect or make a new instrument of government of any higher education corporation in place of the instrument prescribed under subsection (2) above; or

(b) modify an instrument made in pursuance of this subsection.

(4) An instrument of government of a higher education corporation—

(a) shall comply with the requirements of Schedule 7A to this Act; and

(b) may make any provision authorised to be made by that Schedule and such other provision as may be necessary or desirable.

(5) An order under subsection (2) or (3) above may make such provision as appears to the Privy Council necessary or desirable to secure continuity in the government of the institution or institutions to which it relates.

(6) The validity of any proceedings of a higher education corporation for which an instrument of government has effect, or of any committee of such a corporation, shall not be affected by a vacancy amongst the members or by any defect in the appointment or nomination of a member.

(7) Every document purporting to be an instrument made or issued by or on behalf of a higher education corporation for which an instrument of government has effect and to be duly executed under the seal of the corporation, or to be signed or executed by a person authorised by the corporation to act in that behalf, shall be received in evidence and be treated, without further proof, as being so made or issued unless the contrary is shown.

(8) In relation to a higher education corporation for which an instrument of government has effect the members of the corporation for the time being shall be known as the board of governors of the institution conducted by the corporation.

(9) The Secretary of State may by order amend or repeal any of paragraphs 3 to 5 and 11 of Schedule 7A to this Act.

(10) In this section and section 124C "the appointed day" means the day appointed under section 94 of the Further and Higher Education Act 1992 for the commencement of section 71 of that Act.

Accounts. 124B.—(1) It shall be the duty of each corporation—

(a) to keep proper accounts and proper records in relation to the accounts; and

(b) to prepare in respect of each financial year of the corporation a statement of accounts.

(2) The statement shall—

(a) give a true and fair account of the state of the corporation's affairs at the end of the financial year and of the corporation's income and expenditure in the financial year; and

(b) comply with any directions given by the higher education funding council as to the information to be contained in the statement, the manner in which the information is to be presented or the methods and principles according to which the statement is to be prepared.

(3) The corporation shall supply a copy of the statement to any person who asks for it and, if the corporation so requires, pays a fee of such amount not exceeding the cost of supply as the corporation thinks fit.

(4) The accounts (including any statement prepared under this section) shall be audited by persons appointed in respect of each financial year by the corporation.

(5) The corporation shall consult, and take into account any advice given by, the Audit Commission for Local Authorities and the National Health Service in England and Wales before appointing any auditor under subsection (4) above in respect of their first financial year.

(6) No person shall be qualified to be appointed auditor under that subsection except—

(a) an individual, or firm, eligible for appointment as a company auditor under section 25 of the Companies Act 1989;

1989 c. 40.

(b) a member of the Chartered Institute of Public Finance and Accountancy; or

(c) a firm each of the members of which is a member of that institute.

(7) In this section, in relation to a corporation—

"the first financial year" means the period commencing with the date on which the corporation is established and ending with the second 31st March following that date; and

"financial year" means that period and each successive period of twelve months.

**Initial and transitional arrangements.**

124C.—(1) The Secretary of State shall be the appointing authority in relation to the appointment of the first members of a corporation established on or after the appointed day and, in determining the number of members to appoint within each variable category of members, he shall secure that at least half of all the members of the corporation as first constituted are independent members.

(2) In subsection (1) above "variable category of members" and "independent members" have the same meaning as in Schedule 7A to this Act.

(3) The following provisions apply where an instrument of government is made under section 124A of this Act for a higher education corporation with respect to which Schedule 7 to this Act has effect.

(4) The instrument shall apply, subject to subsection (5) below, as if the persons who, immediately before its coming into effect, were the members of the corporation had been appointed in accordance with the instrument for the residue of the term of their then subsisting appointment.

(5) Any local authority nominee, teacher nominee, general staff nominee or student nominee (within the meaning, in each case, of Schedule 7 to this Act) shall cease to hold office.

Exercise of Powers by Privy Council.

124D.—(1) This section applies in relation to the exercise of powers for the purposes of this Part of this Act.

(2) A power vested in the Privy Council may be exercised by any two or more of the lords and others of the Council.

(3) An act of the Privy Council shall be sufficiently signified by an instrument signed by the clerk of the Council.

(4) An order or act signified by an instrument purporting to be signed by the clerk of the Council shall be deemed to have been duly made or done by the Privy Council.

(5) An instrument so signed shall be received in evidence in all courts and proceedings without proof of the authority or signature of the clerk of the Council or other proof."

(2) In section 125 of that Act (articles of government) for "the Secretary of State" (in each place where it appears) there is substituted "the Privy Council"; but nothing in this subsection requires further approval to be given for anything approved by the Secretary of State under that section before the commencement of this subsection.

(3) In Schedule 7 to that Act (constitution of higher education corporations)—

(a) at the end of paragraph 7 (appointments) there is added—

"(8) If the number of independent members of the corporation falls below the number needed in accordance with its articles of government for a quorum, the Secretary of State is the appointing authority in relation to the appointment of such number of independent members as is required for a quorum", and

(b) in paragraph 18 (accounts) after sub-paragraph (2) there is inserted—

"(2A) The corporation shall supply a copy of the statement to any person who asks for it and, if the corporation so requires, pays a fee of such amount not exceeding the cost of supply as the corporation thinks fit."

(4) After that Schedule there is inserted the Schedule set out in Schedule 6 to this Act.

Further power of designation.
1988 c. 40.

**72.**—(1) In section 129 of the Education Reform Act 1988 (designation of institutions)—

(a) for subsections (1) and (2) there is substituted—

"(1) The Secretary of State may by order designate as an institution eligible to receive support from funds administered by a higher education funding council—

(a) any institution which appears to him to fall within subsection (2) below; and

(b) any institution which is, or is to be, conducted by a successor company to a higher education corporation.

(2) An institution falls within this subsection if its full-time equivalent enrolment number for courses of higher education exceeds 55 per cent. of its total full-time equivalent enrolment number", and

(b) subsections (3) and (4) of that section are omitted.

(2) An order in force immediately before the commencement of subsection (1) above designating an institution as falling within subsection (3) of that section shall have effect as if made under that section as amended by subsection (1) above.

(3) In this Part of this Act "designated institution" means an institution in relation to which a designation made, or having effect as if made, under section 129 of that Act has effect.

**73.**—(1) After section 129 of the Education Reform Act 1988 there is inserted—

"Government and conduct of designated institutions.

129A.—(1) This section has effect in relation to any designated institution, other than an institution conducted by a company.

(2) For each such institution there shall be—

(a) an instrument providing for the constitution of a governing body of the institution (to be known as the instrument of government); and

(b) an instrument in accordance with which the institution is to be conducted (to be known as the articles of government),

each of which meets the requirements of subsection (3) below.

(3) Those requirements are that the instrument—

(a) was in force when the designation took effect; or

(b) is made in pursuance of a power under a regulatory instrument, or is made under subsection (5) below,

and is approved for the purposes of this section by the Privy Council.

(4) In this section "regulatory instrument", in relation to an institution, means any instrument of government or articles of government and any other instrument relating to or regulating the institution.

(5) Where there is no such power as is mentioned in subsection (3)(b) above to make the instrument, it may be made by the body of persons responsible for the management of the institution and an instrument made by them under this subsection may replace wholly or partly any existing regulatory instrument.

(6) If an instrument approved by the Privy Council for the purposes of this section—

(a) falls within subsection (3)(a) above or was made in pursuance of a power under a regulatory instrument and, apart from this section, there is no power to modify it; or

(b) was made by the body of persons responsible for the management of the institution,

the instrument may be modified by those persons.

(7) Either of the instruments referred to in subsection (2) above may be modified by order of the Privy Council and no instrument approved by the Privy Council for the purposes of this section may be modified by any other person without the Privy Council's consent.

(8) Before exercising any power under subsection (7) above in relation to any instrument the Privy Council shall consult—

(a) the governing body of the institution, and

(b) where there is such a power as is mentioned in subsection (3)(b) above to modify the instrument and the persons having that power are different from the governing body of the institution, the persons having the power,

so far as it appears to them to be practicable to do so.

(9) Nothing in this section requires further approval for any instrument approved by the Secretary of State for the purposes of section 156 of this Act, and references in this section to instruments approved by the Privy Council for the purposes of this section include instruments so approved by the Secretary of State.

(10) In this section and section 129B "designated institution" means an institution in relation to which a designation made, or having effect as if made, under section 129 of this Act has effect but does not include any institution established by Royal Charter.

Designated institutions conducted by companies.

129B.—(1) This section has effect in relation to any designated institution conducted by a company.

(2) The articles of association of the company shall incorporate—

(a) provision with respect to the constitution of a governing body of the institution (to be known as the instrument of government of the institution); and

(b) provision with respect to the conduct of the institution (to be known as the articles of government of the institution).

(3) The Privy Council may give to the persons who appear to them to have effective control over the company such directions as they think fit for securing that—

    (a)  the memorandum or articles of association of the company; or

    (b)  any rules or bye-laws made in pursuance of any power conferred by the articles of association of the company,

are amended in such manner as they may specify in the direction.

(4) No amendment of the memorandum or articles of association of the company (other than one required under subsection (3)(a) above) shall take effect until it has been submitted to the Privy Council for their approval and they have notified their approval to the company.

(5) Before giving any directions under subsection (3) above the Privy Council shall consult the persons who appear to them to have effective control over the company."

(2) Section 156 of that Act (government and conduct of certain further and higher education institutions) shall cease to have effect in relation to designated institutions.

**74.**—(1) After section 122 of the Education Reform Act 1988 (orders incorporating higher education institutions maintained by local education authorities) there is inserted— '

Transfer of further education institutions to higher education sector.
1988 c. 40.

"Orders transferring further education corporations to higher education sector.

122A.—(1) The Secretary of State may by order provide for the transfer of a further education corporation to the higher education sector if it appears to him that the full-time equivalent enrolment number of the institution conducted by the corporation for courses of higher education exceeds 55 per cent. of its total full-time equivalent enrolment number.

(2) Where an order under this section is made in respect of a further education corporation, sections 124A and 125 of this Act shall have effect as if—

    (a)  on the date the order has effect, the corporation were established as a higher education corporation, and

    (b)  the Secretary of State were the appointing authority in relation to the first members of the higher education corporation.

(3) In determining in pursuance of subsection (2)(b) above the number of members to appoint within each variable category of members, the Secretary of State shall secure that at least half of all the members of the higher education corporation as first constituted are independent members; and in this subsection "variable category of members" and "independent members" have the same meaning as in Schedule 7A to this Act.

(4) On such date as may be specified in the order the corporation shall cease to be a further education corporation and become a higher education corporation and any member of the further education corporation

PART II

who is not re-appointed by the Secretary of State in pursuance of subsection (2)(b) above shall cease to hold office on that date."

1988 c. 40.

(2) An order under section 129 of the Education Reform Act 1988 (designation of institutions for the purposes of the higher education sector) in respect of any institution may revoke any order in respect of that institution under section 28 of this Act.

Variation of trust deeds.

**75.** In section 157 of the Education Reform Act 1988 (variation of trust deeds, etc.) for subsections (1) to (3) (variations by Secretary of State in connection with institutions in the higher education sector or designated assisted institutions) there is substituted—

"(1) An order of the Privy Council may modify any trust deed or other instrument—

(a) relating to or regulating any such institution as is mentioned in subsection (2) below; or

(b) relating to any land or other property held by any person for the purposes of any such institution.

(2) The institutions referred to in subsection (1) above are—

(a) any institution conducted by a higher education corporation; and

(b) any institution in relation to which a designation made, or having effect as if made, under section 129 of this Act has effect, other than an institution established by Royal Charter.

(3) Before making any modifications under subsection (1) above of any trust deed or other instrument the Privy Council shall so far as it appears to them to be practicable to do so consult—

(a) the governing body of the institution;

(b) where that deed or instrument, or any other instrument relating to or regulating the institution concerned, confers power on any other persons to modify or replace that deed or instrument, those persons; and

(c) where the instrument to be modified is a trust deed and the trustees are different from the persons mentioned in paragraphs (a) and (b) above, the trustees."

Power to award degrees, etc.

**76.**—(1) The Privy Council may by order specify any institution which provides higher education as competent to grant in pursuance of this section either or both of the kinds of award mentioned in subsection (2)(a) and (b) below.

(2) The kinds of award referred to in subsection (1) above are—

(a) awards granted to persons who complete an appropriate course of study and satisfy an appropriate assessment, and

   (b) awards granted to persons who complete an appropriate programme of supervised research and satisfy an appropriate assessment,

and in this section "award" means any degree, diploma, certificate or other academic award or distinction and "assessment" includes examination and test.

   (3) An institution for the time being specified in such an order may grant any award of a kind mentioned in subsection (2)(a) or (b) above which it is competent to grant by virtue of the order to persons who complete the appropriate course of study or, as the case may be, programme of supervised research on or after the date specified in the order.

   (4) An institution specified in such an order may also—

     (a) grant honorary degrees, and

     (b) grant degrees to members of the academic and other staff of the institution.

   (5) Any power conferred on an institution to grant awards in pursuance of this section includes power—

     (a) to authorise other institutions to do so on behalf of the institution,

     (b) to do so jointly with another institution, and

     (c) to deprive any person of any award granted to him by or on behalf of the institution in pursuance of this section (or, in the case of an award granted to him by the institution and another institution jointly, to do so jointly with the other institution).

   (6) It shall be for the institution to determine in accordance with any relevant provisions of the instruments relating to or regulating the institution the courses of study or programmes of research, and the assessments, which are appropriate for the grant of any award and the terms and conditions on which any of the powers conferred under this section may be exercised.

   (7) Section 124D of the Education Reform Act 1988 applies in relation to orders under subsection (1) above as it applies in relation to the exercise of powers for the purposes of Part II of that Act.

*1988 c. 40.*

   **77.**—(1) Where—

     (a) power is conferred by any enactment or instrument to change the name of any educational institution or any body corporate carrying on such an institution, and

     (b) the educational institution is within the higher education sector,

then, if the power is exercisable with the consent of the Privy Council, it may (whether or not the institution would apart from this section be a university) be exercised with the consent of the Privy Council so as to include the word "university" in the name of the institution and, if it is carried on by a body corporate, in the name of the body.

Use of "university" in title of institution.

541325 C

(2) The reference in subsection (1) above to a power to change the name of an institution or body includes any power (however expressed and whether or not subject to any conditions or restrictions) in the exercise of which the name of the institution or body may be changed; but the power as extended by that subsection has effect subject to any such conditions or restrictions.

(3) In exercising any power exercisable by virtue of this section to consent to a change in any name the Privy Council shall have regard to the need to avoid names which are or may be confusing.

(4) Any educational institution whose name includes the word "university" by virtue of the exercise of any power as extended by subsection (1) above is to be treated as a university for all purposes.

Financial years of higher education corporations.

**78.**—(1) If the Secretary of State directs that any financial year specified in the direction of the higher education corporations, and subsequent financial years, are to begin with a date specified in the direction, then—

(a) the financial year of the corporations immediately preceding the year specified in the direction shall end immediately before the date specified in the direction, and

(b) the financial year specified in the direction and subsequent financial years shall be each successive period of twelve months.

1988 c. 40.

(2) Section 124B(7) of, and paragraph 18 of Schedule 7 to, the Education Reform Act 1988 (financial years) shall have effect subject to this section.

*General*

Duty to give information to the funding councils.

**79.** Each of the following shall give a council such information as they may require for the purposes of the exercise of any of their functions under the Education Acts—

(a) a local education authority,

(b) the governing body of any institution within the higher education sector, and

(c) the governing body of any institution at which prescribed courses of higher education are currently or have at any time been provided.

Dissolution of Council for National Academic Awards.

**80.**—(1) The Secretary of State may by order provide—

(a) for the dissolution of the Council for National Academic Awards, and

(b) for all property, rights and liabilities to which the Council is entitled or subject immediately before the order comes into force to become property, rights and liabilities of such person as may be specified in the order.

(2) If the order so provides the person so specified shall discharge any duty relating to accounts and records under the statutes of the Council for National Academic Awards in respect of any period ending before the dissolution of the council which would have fallen to be discharged by the council after the dissolution or fell to be so discharged before the dissolution but has not been discharged.

**81.**—(1) In exercising their functions under this Part of this Act, each council shall comply with any directions under this section, and such directions shall be contained in an order made by the Secretary of State.

(2) The Secretary of State may give general directions to a council about the exercise of their functions.

(3) If it appears to the Secretary of State that the financial affairs of any institution within the higher education sector have been or are being mismanaged he may, after consulting the council and the institution, give such directions to the council about the provision of financial support in respect of the activities carried on by the institution as he considers are necessary or expedient by reason of the mismanagement.

# PART III

## MISCELLANEOUS AND GENERAL

**82.**—(1) Any two or more councils may exercise jointly any of their functions where it appears to them that to do so—

(a) will be more efficient, or

(b) will enable them more effectively to discharge any of their functions.

(2) Any two or more councils shall, if directed to do so by the Secretary of State, jointly make provision for the assessment by a person appointed by them of matters relating to the arrangements made by each institution in Great Britain which is within the higher education sector for maintaining academic standards in the institution.

(3) In this section—

(a) "council" means a higher education funding council, a further education funding council or the Scottish Higher Education Funding Council, and

(b) references to institutions within the higher education sector include institutions within the higher education sector within the meaning of Part II of the Further and Higher Education (Scotland) Act 1992.

**83.**—(1) A further education funding council or a higher education funding council may arrange for the promotion or carrying out by any person of studies designed to improve economy, efficiency and effectiveness in the management or operations of an institution within the further education sector or, as the case may be, the higher education sector.

(2) A person promoting or carrying out such studies at the request of a council may require the governing body of the institution concerned—

(a) to furnish the person, or any person authorised by him, with such information, and

(b) to make available to him, or any person so authorised, for inspection their accounts and such other documents,

as the person may reasonably require for that purpose.

PART III
Effect of
agreements made
before date of
transfer.
1988 c. 40.

**84.**—(1) This section applies where—

(a) (apart from this section) any land or other property of a local authority would on any date ("the date of transfer") be transferred under Part I of this Act or Part II of the Education Reform Act 1988 to the governing body of an institution within the further education sector or the higher education sector, and

(b) at any time before that date the authority, the governing body of the institution and the governing body of any other institution which will on that date be an institution within the further education sector or the higher education sector have agreed in writing that the land or property should be transferred on that or a subsequent date to the governing body of that other institution.

(2) If the Secretary of State has approved the agreement at any time before the date of transfer, Part I of this Act or, as the case may be, Part II of the Education Reform Act 1988 shall have effect as if they required the property to be transferred in accordance with the agreement.

(3) References in this section to anything done include anything done before the passing of this Act.

Finance and
government of
locally funded
further and higher
education.

**85.**—(1) Chapter III of Part II of the Education Reform Act 1988 (finance and government of locally funded further and higher education) shall cease to have effect; and section 156 of that Act (government and conduct of certain further and higher education institutions) shall cease to have effect in relation to designated assisted institutions.

(2) A local education authority shall have the following powers in relation to any institution, not within the further education sector or the higher education sector, which is maintained by them in the exercise of their further or higher education functions.

(3) The authority may—

(a) make such provision as they think fit in respect of the government of the institution (including replacing any instrument of government or articles of government of the institution made under that Chapter or that section), and

(b) delegate to the governing body of the institution such functions relating to the management of the finances of the institution, and such other functions relating to the management of the institution (including the appointment and dismissal of staff), as the authority may determine.

Temporary
exclusion of
section 5 of Data
Protection Act
1984 in relation to
data transferred to
new bodies.
1984 c. 35.

**86.**—(1) Where personal data are transferred under any provision of this Act to a body corporate established under this Act, section 5(1) of the Data Protection Act 1984 (prohibition of unregistered holding, etc, of personal data) shall not apply in relation to the holding by that body corporate of the data so transferred or any data of the same description as the data so transferred until the end of the period of six months beginning—

(a) in the case of a body established to conduct an educational institution, the date on which the body begins to conduct the institution, and

(b) in any other case, when the body is established.

(2) Expressions used in subsection (1) above and in that Act have the same meaning in that subsection as in that Act.

PART III

**87.** Schedule 7 to this Act has effect to supplement the provisions of this Act relating to the transfer of property, rights and liabilities.

Transfers of property, etc: supplementary provision.

**88.**—(1) Subject to subsection (2) below, stamp duty shall not be chargeable in respect of any transfer effected under or by virtue of any of the following sections of this Act: 23, 25, 27, 32, 34, 40(5) and (7), 63 and 80.

Stamp duty.

(2) No instrument (other than a statutory instrument) made or executed under or in pursuance of any of the provisions mentioned in subsection (1) shall be treated as duly stamped unless it is stamped with the duty to which it would, but for this section (and, if applicable, section 129 of the Finance Act 1982), be liable or it has, in accordance with the provisions of section 12 of the Stamp Act 1891, been stamped with a particular stamp denoting that it is not chargeable with any duty or that it has been duly stamped.

1982 c. 39.
1891 c. 39.

**89.**—(1) Any power of the Secretary of State to make orders or regulations under this Act (other than under any of the excepted provisions) shall be exercised by statutory instrument.

Orders, regulations and directions.

(2) For the purposes of subsection (1) above the excepted provisions are sections 22, 29(6) and (8), 38, 46 and 57; but section 14 of the Interpretation Act 1978 (implied power to amend) applies to orders made under those sections as it applies to orders made by statutory instrument.

1978 c. 30.

(3) A statutory instrument containing any order or regulations under this Act, other than an order under section 94, shall be subject to annulment in pursuance of a resolution of either House of Parliament.

(4) Orders or regulations under this Act may make different provision for different cases, circumstances or areas and may contain such incidental, supplemental, saving or transitional provisions as the Secretary of State thinks fit.

(5) Section 111 of the Education Act 1944 (revocation and variation) applies to directions given under this Act as it applies to directions given under that Act.

1944 c. 31.

**90.**—(1) In this Act—

Interpretation.

"contract of employment", "employee" and "employer" have the same meaning as in the Employment Protection (Consolidation) Act 1978, and "employed" means employed under a contract of employment,

1978 c. 44.

"the Education Acts" means the Education Acts 1944 to 1992,

"governing body", in relation to an institution, means, subject to subsection (2) below—

(a) in the case of an institution conducted by a further education corporation or a higher education corporation, the corporation,

(b) in the case of a university not falling within paragraph (a) above, the executive governing body which has responsibility for the management and administration of its revenue and property and the conduct of its affairs,

(c) in the case of any other institution not falling within paragraph (a) or (b) above for which there is an instrument of government providing for the constitution of a governing body, the governing body so provided for, and

(d) in any other case, any board of governors of the institution or any persons responsible for the management of the institution, whether or not formally constituted as a governing body or board of governors,

1988 c. 40.

"higher education" has the same meaning as in the Education Reform Act 1988,

"higher education corporation" means a body corporate established under section 121 or 122 of the Education Reform Act 1988, including those sections as applied by section 227(4) of that Act (application to Wales), or a body corporate which has become a higher education corporation by virtue of section 122A of that Act,

"interest in land" includes any easement, right or charge in, to or over land,

"land" includes buildings and other structures, land covered with water and any interest in land,

"liability" includes obligation, and

"local authority" means a county council, a district council, a London borough council or (in their capacity as a local authority) the Common Council of the City of London.

(2) The Secretary of State may by order provide for any reference in the Education Acts to the governing body of an institution, in relation to an institution which is—

(a) a designated institution for the purposes of Part I or Part II of this Act, and

(b) conducted by a company,

to be read as a reference to the governing body provided for in the instrument of government, or to the company or to both.

(3) In this Act "university" includes a university college and any college, or institution in the nature of a college, in a university; but where a college or institution would not, apart from this subsection, fall to be treated separately it shall not be so treated for the purpose of determining whether any institution is in England or in Wales.

(4) References in this Act to institutions within the PCFC funding sector are to be construed in accordance with section 132(6) of the Education Reform Act 1988.

(5) Subject to the provisions of this Act, expressions used in this Act and in the Education Act 1944 have the same meaning in this Act as in that Act.

1944 c. 31.

Interpretation of Education Acts.

**91.**—(1) This section applies for the interpretation of the Education Acts.

(2) References to a further education funding council are to a council established under section 1 of this Act.

(3) References to institutions within the further education sector are to—

    (a) institutions conducted by further education corporations, and

    (b) designated institutions for the purposes of Part I of this Act (defined in section 28(4) of this Act),

and references to institutions outside the further education sector are to be read accordingly.

(4) References to a higher education funding council are to a council established under section 62 of this Act, subject to subsection (6) of that section.

(5) References to institutions within the higher education sector are to—

    (a) universities receiving financial support under section 65 of this Act,

    (b) institutions conducted by higher education corporations, and

    (c) designated institutions for the purposes of Part II of this Act (defined in section 72(3) of this Act),

and references to institutions outside the higher education sector are to be read accordingly.

(6) References, in relation to a further education corporation or higher education corporation, to the institution—

    (a) in relation to any time before the operative date for the purposes of Part I of this Act (defined in section 17 of this Act) or, as the case may be, the transfer date for the purposes of the Education Reform Act 1988 (defined in section 123 of that Act), are to the institution the corporation is established to conduct, and

    (b) in relation to any later time or to any corporation which is a further education corporation by virtue of section 47 of this Act or a higher education corporation by virtue of section 122A of that Act, are to any institution for the time being conducted by the corporation in the exercise of their powers under this or that Act.

1988 c. 40.

PART III

Index.

**92.** The expressions listed in the left-hand column below are respectively defined by or (as the case may be) are to be interpreted in accordance with the provisions of this Act listed in the right-hand column in relation to those expressions.

| *Expression* | *Relevant provision* |
|---|---|
| appropriate further education funding council | section 1(6) |
| contract of employment, etc. | section 90(1) |
| council (in Part I), or further education funding council | sections 1(5) and 91(2) |
| council (in Part II), or higher education funding council | sections 61(3)(b), 62(5) and (6) and 91(4) |
| designated institution (in Part I) | section 28(4) |
| designated institution (in Part II) | section 72(3) |
| the Education Acts | section 90(1) |
| functions | section 61(1) |
| further education | section 14(1) to (4) |
| further education corporation | section 17(1) |
| governing body | section 90(1) and (2) |
| higher education | section 90(1) |
| higher education corporation | section 90(1) |
| institution in England or in Wales (in relation to higher education funding councils) | section 62(7) |
| institutions within or outside the further education sector | section 91(3) |
| institutions within or outside the higher education sector | sections 61(3)(a) and 91(5) |
| institutions within the PCFC funding sector | section 90(4) |
| interest in land | section 90(1) |
| land | section 90(1) |
| liability | section 90(1) |
| local authority | section 90(1) |
| modification | section 61(1) |
| operative date | sections 17 and 33(4) |
| pupil | section 14(6) |
| regulations | section 61(1) |
| secondary education | section 14(2) to (4) |
| school | section 14(5) |
| transfer of rights or liabilities | section 61(2) |
| university | section 90(3) |

Amendments and repeals.

**93.**—(1) Schedule 8 (which makes minor and consequential amendments) shall have effect.

(2) The enactments mentioned in Schedule 9 to this Act are repealed to the extent mentioned in the third column.

Short title, commencement, etc.
1991 c. 49.

**94.**—(1) This Act may be cited as the Further and Higher Education Act 1992.

(2) The Education Acts 1944 to 1990, the School Teachers' Pay and Conditions Act 1991 and this Act may be cited together as the Education Acts 1944 to 1992.

(3)  This Act shall come into force on such day as the Secretary of State may by order appoint and different days may be appointed for different provisions and for different purposes.

(4)  Subject to the following provisions of this section, this Act extends to England and Wales only.

(5)  Sections 63, 64 and 82 of this Act extend also to Scotland.

(6)  Section 80 extends also to Scotland and Northern Ireland.

(7)  The amendment by this Act of an enactment which extends to Scotland or Northern Ireland extends also to Scotland or, as the case may be, Northern Ireland.

# SCHEDULES

Sections 1, 9, 62 and 70.

## SCHEDULE 1

### THE FURTHER AND HIGHER EDUCATION FUNDING COUNCILS

#### *Supplementary powers*

1.—(1) Subject to sub-paragraph (2) below, the council may do anything which appears to them to be necessary or expedient for the purpose of or in connection with the discharge of their functions, including in particular—

    (a) acquiring and disposing of land and other property,

    (b) entering into contracts,

    (c) investing sums not immediately required for the purpose of the discharge of their functions, and

    (d) accepting gifts of money, land or other property.

(2) The council shall not borrow money.

#### *Chief officer*

2.—(1) One of the members of the council shall be the chief officer.

(2) The first chief officer shall be appointed as such by the Secretary of State and shall hold and vacate office in accordance with the terms of his appointment.

(3) Each subsequent chief officer shall be appointed by the council with the approval of the Secretary of State on such terms and conditions (including terms with respect to tenure and vacation of office) as the council may with the approval of the Secretary of State determine.

(4) On approval by the Secretary of State of the person to be appointed on any occasion as chief officer of the council and the terms and conditions of his appointment, the Secretary of State shall—

    (a) if that person is not already a member of the council, appoint him as a member for the same term as the term of his appointment as chief officer, or

    (b) if he is already such a member but his term of appointment as such ends before the term of his appointment as chief officer ends, extend his term of appointment as a member so that it ends at the same time as the term of his appointment as chief officer.

#### *Tenure of members of councils*

3.—(1) A person shall hold and vacate office as a member or as chairman or chief officer of the council in accordance with the terms of his appointment and shall, on ceasing to be a member, be eligible for re-appointment.

(2) A person may at any time by notice in writing to the Secretary of State resign his office as a member or as chairman of the council.

4. If the Secretary of State is satisfied that a member of the council—

    (a) has been absent from meetings of the council for a period longer than six consecutive months without the permission of the council, or

    (b) is unable or unfit to discharge the functions of a member,

the Secretary of State may by notice in writing to that member remove him from office and thereupon the office shall become vacant.

*Salaries, allowances and pensions*

5.—(1) The council—

   (a) shall pay to their members such salaries or fees, and such travelling, subsistence or other allowances, as the Secretary of State may determine, and

   (b) shall, as regards any member in whose case the Secretary of State may so determine, pay or make provision for the payment of such sums by way of pension, allowances and gratuities to or in respect of him as the Secretary of State may determine.

(2) If a person ceases to be a member of the council and it appears to the Secretary of State that there are special circumstances which make it right that he should receive compensation, the Secretary of State may direct the council to make to that person a payment of such amount as the Secretary of State may determine.

(3) The council shall pay to the members of any of their committees who are not members of the council such travelling, subsistence and other allowances as the Secretary of State may determine.

(4) A determination or direction of the Secretary of State under this paragraph requires the approval of the Treasury.

*House of Commons disqualification*

6. In Part III of Schedule 1 to the House of Commons Disqualification Act 1975 (disqualifying offices) there are inserted at the appropriate places— 1975 c. 24.

   "Any member of the Further Education Funding Council for England in receipt of remuneration.

   Any member of the Further Education Funding Council for Wales in receipt of remuneration.

   Any member of the Higher Education Funding Council for England in receipt of remuneration.

   Any member of the Higher Education Funding Council for Wales in receipt of remuneration."

*Staff*

7.—(1) The council may appoint such employees as they think fit.

(2) The council shall pay to their employees such remuneration and allowances as the council may determine.

(3) The employees shall be appointed on such other terms and conditions as the council may determine.

(4) A determination under sub-paragraph (2) or (3) above requires the approval of the Secretary of State given with the consent of the Treasury.

(5) Employment with the council shall be included among the kinds of employment to which a scheme under section 1 of the Superannuation Act 1972 can apply, and accordingly in Schedule 1 to that Act (in which those kinds of employment are listed), at the end of the list of "Other Bodies" there is inserted— 1972 c. 11.

   "Further Education Funding Council for England.

   Further Education Funding Council for Wales.

   Higher Education Funding Council for England.

   Higher Education Funding Council for Wales."

(6) The council shall pay to the Treasury, at such times as the Treasury may direct, such sums as the Treasury may determine in respect of the increase attributable to sub-paragraph (5) above in the sums payable out of money provided by Parliament under that Act.

(7) Where an employee of the council is, by reference to that employment, a participant in a scheme under section 1 of that Act and is also a member of the council, the Treasury may determine that his service as such a member shall be treated for the purposes of the scheme as service as an employee of the council (whether or not any benefits are payable to or in respect of him by virtue of paragraph 5 above).

### *Committees*

8.—(1) The council may establish a committee for any purpose.

(2) The number of the members of a committee established under this paragraph, and the terms on which they are to hold and vacate office, shall be fixed by the council.

(3) Such a committee may include persons who are not members of the council.

(4) The council shall keep under review the structure of committees established under this paragraph and the scope of each committee's activities.

### *Further Education Funding Council for England: regional committees*

9.—(1) There shall be established for each region of England determined by the Secretary of State a committee of the Further Education Funding Council for England to advise the council on such matters relating to the facilities for the population of the region—

   (a) for further education, or

   (b) for full-time education (other than further education) suitable to the requirements of persons over compulsory school age who have not attained the age of nineteen years,

as the council may from time to time require.

(2) The number of the members of a committee established under this paragraph shall be determined by the Secretary of State and he shall appoint the members of the committee.

(3) Paragraphs 3 and 4 above apply to members of a committee established under this paragraph as they apply to members of a council.

### *Delegation of Functions*

10. The council may authorise the chairman, the chief officer or any committee established under paragraph 8 above to exercise such of their functions as they may determine.

### *Proceedings*

11. Without prejudice to any other rights the Secretary of State may require to be accorded to him as a condition of any grants made to the council under this Act—

   (a) a representative of the Secretary of State shall be entitled to attend and take part in any deliberations (but not in decisions) at meetings of the council or of any committee of the council, and

   (b) the council shall provide the Secretary of State with such copies of any documents distributed to members of the council or of any such committee as he may require.

12. The validity of any proceedings of the council or of any committee of the council shall not be affected by a vacancy among the members or by any defect in the appointment of a member.

13. Subject to the preceding provisions of this Schedule, the council may regulate their own procedure and that of any of their committees.

### *Application of seal and proof of instruments*

14. The application of the seal of the council shall be authenticated by the signature—

   (a) of the chairman or of some other person authorised either generally or specially by the council to act for that purpose, and

   (b) of one other member.

15. Every document purporting to be an instrument made or issued by or on behalf of the council and to be duly executed under the seal of the council, or to be signed or executed by a person authorised by the council to act in that behalf, shall be received in evidence and be treated, without further proof, as being so made or issued unless the contrary is shown.

### *Accounts*

16.—(1) It shall be the duty of the council—

   (a) to keep proper accounts and proper records in relation to the accounts,

   (b) to prepare in respect of each financial year of the council a statement of accounts, and

   (c) to send copies of the statement to the Secretary of State and to the Comptroller and Auditor General before the end of the month of August next following the financial year to which the statement relates.

(2) The statement of accounts shall comply with any directions given by the Secretary of State with the approval of the Treasury as to—

   (a) the information to be contained in it,

   (b) the manner in which the information contained in it is to be presented, or

   (c) the methods and principles according to which the statement is to be prepared,

and shall contain such additional information as the Secretary of State may with the approval of the Treasury require to be provided for the information of Parliament.

(3) The Comptroller and Auditor General shall examine, certify and report on each statement received by him in pursuance of this paragraph and shall lay copies of each statement and of his report before each House of Parliament.

(4) In this paragraph "financial year" means the period beginning with the date on which the council is established and ending with the second 31st March following that date, and each successive period of twelve months.

### *Status of council*

17. The council shall not be regarded as the servant or agent of the Crown or as enjoying any status, immunity or privilege of the Crown; and the property of the council shall not be regarded as property of, or property held on behalf of, the Crown.

541325 D

# SCHEDULE 2

## COURSES OF FURTHER EDUCATION

The descriptions of courses of further education referred to in section 3(1) of this Act are the following—

(a) a course which prepares students to obtain a vocational qualification which is, or falls within a class, for the time being approved for the purposes of this sub-paragraph by the Secretary of State,

(b) a course which prepares students to qualify for—

(i) the General Certificate of Secondary Education, or

(ii) the General Certificate of Education at Advanced Level or Advanced Supplementary Level (including Special Papers),

(c) a course for the time being approved for the purposes of this sub-paragraph by the Secretary of State which prepares students for entry to a course of higher education,

(d) a course which prepares students for entry to another course falling within paragraphs (a) to (c) above,

(e) a course for basic literacy in English,

(f) a course to improve the knowledge of English of those for whom English is not the language spoken at home,

(g) a course to teach the basic principles of mathematics,

(h) in relation to Wales, a course for proficiency or literacy in Welsh,

(j) a course to teach independent living and communication skills to persons having learning difficulties which prepares them for entry to another course falling within paragraphs (d) to (h) above.

# SCHEDULE 3

## CALCULATION OF ENROLMENT NUMBERS

### *Enrolment numbers*

1.—(1) The enrolment number for any institution at any time is the aggregate of—

(a) the number of full-time students enrolled at that institution at that time to follow courses of further or higher education, and

(b) the numbers arrived at under sub-paragraph (3) below for each mode of attendance at such courses specified in the first three entries in column 1 of the table in paragraph 2 below.

(2) The total enrolment number for any institution at any time is the aggregate of—

(a) the number of full-time students enrolled at that institution at that time to follow courses of further or higher education, and

(b) the numbers arrived at under sub-paragraph (3) below for each mode of attendance at such courses specified in column 1 of the table in paragraph 2 below.

(3) The number for any mode of attendance at a course is that arrived at by multiplying by the appropriate multiplier the number of students enrolled at the institution at the time in question to follow the course by that mode of attendance.

(4) In sub-paragraph (3) above "the appropriate multiplier" means, in relation to a mode of attendance, the figure given in relation to that mode of attendance in column 2 of the table.

*Table for calculating enrolment numbers for sandwich courses, etc.*

2. The following table applies for the purpose of determining the numbers mentioned in paragraph 1(1)(b) and (2)(b) above—

| (1) Mode of attendance | (2) Multiplier |
|---|---|
| 1. Sandwich course | 0.7 |
| 2. Block release | 1.0 |
| 3. Day release | 0.3 |
| 4. Part-time (other than day release but including some day-time study) | 0.2 |
| 5. Part-time (evening only study) | 0.1 |
| 6. Open or distance learning | 0.075 |

*Interpretation of paragraphs 1 and 2*

3.—(1) For the purposes of paragraph 1(1)(a) and (2)(a) above a student is a full-time student in relation to a course of any description if all his studies for the purposes of that course are full-time studies.

(2) For the purposes of paragraph 2 above—

(a) a student's mode of attendance at a course of any description is by way of a sandwich course if—

(i) in following that course, he engages in periods of full-time study for the purposes of the course alternating with periods of full-time work experience which form part of that course, and

(ii) his average period of full-time study for the purposes of the course for each academic year included in the course is nineteen weeks or more,

(b) a student's mode of attendance at a course of any description is by way of block release if—

(i) the course involves a period of full-time study interrupted by a period of industrial training or employment (whether or not it also includes study on one or two days a week during any other period), and

(ii) his average period of full-time study for the purposes of the course for each academic year included in the course is less than nineteen weeks,

(c) a student's mode of attendance at a course of any description is by way of day release if—

(i) he is in employment, and

(ii) he is released by his employer to follow that course during any part of the working week, and

(d) a student's mode of attendance at a course of any description is by way of open or distance learning if—

(i) he is provided for the purposes of the course with learning material for private study, and

                (ii) his written work for the purposes of the course is subject to a marking and comment service provided for students following the course by private study (whether or not any additional advisory or teaching services are also provided for such students as part of the course).

### *Amendment of paragraphs 1 to 3*

4. The Secretary of State may by order amend paragraphs 1 to 3 above except so far as they apply for calculating an institution's enrolment number, or total enrolment number, on 1st November 1990.

### *Exclusion of non-EEC students*

5. For the purpose of calculating under those paragraphs any enrolment number at any time of any institution, any student enrolled at the institution whose ordinary place of residence then was or is in a country or territory other than a member State shall be disregarded.

Section 20.
## SCHEDULE 4

### INSTRUMENTS AND ARTICLES OF GOVERNMENT FOR FURTHER EDUCATION CORPORATIONS

1. References in this Schedule to an instrument are to an instrument of government or articles of government.

2.—(1) An instrument shall provide for the number of members of the further education corporation, the eligibility of persons for membership and the appointment of members.

(2) An instrument may provide for the nomination of any person for membership by another, including by a body nominated by the Secretary of State.

3. An instrument shall provide for one or more officers to be chosen from among the members.

4. An instrument may provide for the corporation to establish committees and permit such committees to include persons who are not members of the corporation.

5. An instrument may provide for the delegation of functions of the corporation to officers or committees.

6. An instrument may provide for the corporation to pay allowances to its members.

7. An instrument shall provide for the authentication of the application of the seal of the corporation.

8. An instrument shall require the corporation to keep proper accounts and proper records in relation to the accounts and to prepare in respect of each financial year of the corporation a statement of accounts.

9. An instrument shall provide for the appointment of a principal of the institution and determine which functions exercisable in relation to the institution are to be exercised by the corporation, its officers or committees and which by the principal of the institution.

10. An instrument shall make provision about the procedures of the corporation and of the institution.

11. An instrument shall provide—

    (a) for the appointment, promotion, suspension and dismissal of staff, and

    (b) for the admission, suspension and expulsion of students.

12. An instrument may make provision authorising the corporation to make rules or bye-laws for the government and conduct of the institution, including in particular rules or bye-laws about the conduct of students, staff or both.

## SCHEDULE 5

IDENTIFICATION AND APPORTIONMENT, ETC., OF PROPERTY

*Division and apportionment of property etc.*

1.—(1) Any property, rights and liabilities of a transferor authority held or used, or subsisting—

    (a) for the purposes of more than one relevant institution, or

    (b) partly for the purposes of one or more relevant institutions and partly for other purposes of the transferor authority,

shall, where the nature of the property, right or liability permits, be divided or apportioned between the transferees, or (as the case may be) between the transferor authority and the transferee or transferees, in such proportions as may be appropriate.

(2) Where any estate or interest in land falls to be so divided—

    (a) any rent payable under a lease in respect of that estate or interest, and

    (b) any rent charged on that estate or interest,

shall be correspondingly divided or apportioned so that each part is payable in respect of, or charged on, only one part of the estate or interest and the other part or parts are payable in respect of, or charged on, only the other part or parts of the estate or interest.

(3) Any property, right or liability held or used, or subsisting, as mentioned in sub-paragraph (1) above the nature of which does not permit its division or apportionment as so mentioned shall be transferred to the transferee (or to one or other of the transferees) or retained by the transferor authority according to—

    (a) in the case of an estate or interest in land, whether on the operative date the transferor authority or the transferee (or one or other of the transferees) appears to be in greater need of the security afforded by that estate or interest or, where none of them appears to be in greater need of that security, which of them appears on that date to be likely to make use of the land to the greater extent, or

SCH. 5

(b) in the case of any other property or any right or liability, which of them appears on the operative date to be likely to make use of the property or (as the case may be) to be affected by the right or liability to the greater extent,

subject (in either case) to such arrangements for the protection of the other person or persons concerned as may be agreed between the transferor authority and the Education Assets Board or determined by the Board under paragraph 3 below.

(4) In this paragraph—

(a) references to a relevant institution are references to—

(i) any institution a body corporate is established under this Act to conduct, and

(ii) any institution in relation to which section 32 of this Act has effect, and

(b) references to a transferor authority are references to a local authority who are the transferor for the purposes of any transfer to which this Schedule applies.

### *Identification of property, rights and liabilities*

2.—(1) It shall be the duty of the transferor and the Education Assets Board, whether before or after the operative date, so far as practicable to arrive at such written agreements, and to execute such other instruments, as are necessary or expedient to identify or define the property, rights and liabilities transferred to the transferee or retained by the transferor or for making any such arrangements as are mentioned in paragraph 1(3) above and as will—

(a) afford to the transferor and the transferee as against one another such rights and safeguards as they may require for the proper discharge of their respective functions, and

(b) make as from such date, not being earlier than the operative date, as may be specified in the agreement or instrument such clarifications and modifications of the effect of the provision of this Act under which the transfer is required on the property, rights and liabilities of the transferor as will best serve the proper discharge of the respective functions of the transferor and the transferee.

(2) Any such agreement or instrument shall provide so far as it is expedient—

(a) for the granting of leases and for the creation of other liabilities and rights over land whether amounting in law to interests in land or not, and whether involving the surrender of any existing interest or the creation of a new interest or not,

(b) for the granting of indemnities in connection with the severance of leases and other matters,

(c) for responsibility for registration of any matter in any description of statutory register.

3.—(1) The Education Assets Board may, in the case of any matter on which agreement is required to be reached under paragraph 2(1) above—

(a) if it appears to them that it is unlikely that such an agreement will be reached, or

(b) if such an agreement has not been reached within such period as may be prescribed by regulations,

give a direction determining that matter, and may include in the direction any provision which might have been included in an agreement under paragraph 2(1).

(2) A direction under sub-paragraph (1) above may be given before or after the operative date.

(3) Any property, rights or liabilities required by a direction under this paragraph to be transferred to the transferee shall be regarded as having been transferred to, and by virtue of this Act vested in, the transferee accordingly.

(4) The Board shall, before giving a direction under this paragraph, give the transferor and the transferee such opportunity as may be prescribed by regulations to make written representations.

4.—(1) The transferor or transferee, if dissatisfied with a determination under paragraph 3 above, may appeal to the Secretary of State.

(2) An appeal under this paragraph shall be made in accordance with regulations.

(3) The Secretary of State shall, before determining an appeal under this paragraph, give the appellant and the respondent such opportunity as may be prescribed by regulations to make written representations.

(4) On an appeal under this paragraph the Secretary of State may—

(a) allow or dismiss the appeal or vary the determination of the Board, and

(b) give a direction accordingly under paragraph 3 above.

5.—(1) Regulations may prescribe the procedure to be followed in making any determination under paragraphs 3 and 4 above.

(2) The regulations may in particular—

(a) provide for a time limit within which written representations and any supporting documents must be submitted,

(b) empower the determining authority to proceed to a determination taking into account only such written representations and supporting documents as were submitted within the time limit, and

(c) empower the determining authority to proceed to a determination, after giving the transferor and the transferee or, as the case may be, the appellant and the respondent written notice of their intention to do so, notwithstanding that no written representations were made within the time limit, if it appears to the determining authority that they have sufficient material before them to enable them to make a determination.

(3) In sub-paragraph (2) above the "determining authority" means the Board or the Secretary of State, as the case may be.

*Documents of title*

6.—(1) Where a transfer to which this Schedule applies relates to registered land, it shall be the duty of the transferor to execute any such instrument under the Land Registration Acts 1925 to 1986, to deliver any such certificate under those Acts and to do such other things under those Acts as he would be required to execute, deliver or do in the case of a transfer by agreement between the transferor and the transferee.

(2) Where on any transfer to which this Schedule applies the transferor is entitled to retain possession of any documents relating in part to the title to any land or other property transferred to the transferee, the transferor shall be treated as having given to the transferee an acknowledgment in writing of the right of the transferee to production of that document and to delivery of copies of it; and section 64 of the Law of Property Act 1925 shall have effect accordingly, and on the basis that the acknowledgment did not contain any such expression of contrary intention as is mentioned in that section.

1925 c. 20.

*Third parties affected by vesting provisions*

7.—(1) Without prejudice to the generality of paragraphs 2 to 4 of Schedule 7 to this Act, any transaction effected between a transferor and a transferee in pursuance of paragraph 2(1) or of a direction under paragraph 3 above shall be binding on all other persons, and notwithstanding that it would, apart from this sub-paragraph, have required the consent or concurrence of any person other than the transferor and the transferee.

(2) If as a result of any such transaction any person's rights or liabilities become enforceable as to part by or against the transferor and as to part by or against the transferee, the Education Assets Board shall give that person written notification of that fact.

(3) If in consequence of a transfer to which this Schedule applies or of anything done in pursuance of the provisions of this Schedule—

(a) the rights or liabilities of any person other than the transferor or the transferee which were enforceable against or by the transferor become enforceable as to part against or by the transferor and as to part against or by the transferee, and

(b) the value of any property or interest of that person is thereby diminished,

such compensation as may be just shall be paid to that person by the transferor, the transferee or both.

(4) Any dispute as to whether and if so how much compensation is payable under sub-paragraph (3) above, or as to the person to whom it shall be paid, shall be referred to and determined by an arbitrator appointed by the Lord Chancellor.

(5) Where the transferor or the transferee under a transfer to which this Schedule applies purports by any conveyance or transfer to transfer to some person other than the transferor or the transferee for consideration any land or other property which before the operative date belonged to the transferor, or which is an interest in property which before that date belonged to the transferor, the conveyance or transfer shall be as effective as if both the transferor and the transferee had been parties to it and had thereby conveyed or transferred all their interest in the property conveyed or transferred.

(6) A court shall have the power set out in sub-paragraph (7) below if at any stage in proceedings before it to which the transferor or transferee under a transfer to which this Schedule applies and a person other than the transferor or the transferee are parties it appears to it that the issues in the proceedings—

(a) depend on the identification or definition of any of the property, rights or liabilities transferred which the transferor and the Education Assets Board have not yet effected, or

(b) raise a question of construction on the relevant provisions of this Act which would not arise if the transferor and the transferee constituted a single person.

(7) In any such case the court may, if it thinks fit on the application of a party to the proceedings other than the transferor or the transferee, hear and determine the proceedings on the footing that such one of the transferor and the transferee as is a party to the proceedings represents and is answerable for the other of them, and that the transferor and the transferee constitute a single person.

(8) Any judgment or order given by a court in proceedings determined on that footing shall bind both the transferor and the transferee accordingly.

(9) It shall be the duty of the transferor and of the Education Assets Board to keep one another informed of any case where the transferor or the transferee under a transfer to which this Schedule applies may be prejudiced by sub-paragraph (5) above or any judgment or order given by virtue of sub-paragraph (8) above.

(10) If either the transferor or the transferee claims that he has been so prejudiced and that the other of them ought to indemnify or make a payment to him on that account and has unreasonably failed to meet that claim, he may refer the matter to the Secretary of State for determination by the Secretary of State.

### *Delivery of documents to transferee*

8. When it appears to the Education Assets Board, in the case of any transfer, that any agreements and instruments required to be made or executed in pursuance of paragraph 2(1) above or in pursuance of a direction under paragraph 3 above have been made or executed, the Board shall deliver those agreements and instruments (if any) to the transferee.

## SCHEDULE 6

Section 71.

### NEW SCHEDULE 7A TO THE EDUCATION REFORM ACT 1988

#### "SCHEDULE 7A

##### INSTRUMENTS OF GOVERNMENT MADE BY PRIVY COUNCIL

### *Name of corporation*

1. The instrument shall empower the corporation to change their name with the consent of the Privy Council.

### *Membership*

2. The instrument shall make provision for the membership of the corporation which meets all the requirements of paragraphs 3 to 5 below.

3.—(1) The corporation shall consist of—

    (a) not less than twelve and not more than twenty-four members appointed in accordance with the following provisions; and

    (b) the person who is for the time being the principal of the institution, unless he chooses not to be a member.

(2) Of the appointed members—

    (a) up to thirteen (referred to below in this Schedule as the "independent members") shall be persons appearing to the appointing authority to have experience of, and to have shown capacity in, industrial, commercial or employment matters or the practice of any profession;

    (b) up to two may be teachers at the institution nominated by the academic board and up to two may be students at the institution nominated by the students at the institution; and

    (c) at least one and not more than nine (referred to below in this Schedule as the "co-opted members") shall be persons nominated by the members of the corporation who are not co-opted members.

(3) The co-opted member required by sub-paragraph (2)(c) above shall be a person who has experience in the provision of education.

(4) A person (other than a person appointed in pursuance of sub-paragraph (2)(b) above) who is—

    (a) employed at the institution (whether or not as a teacher);

    (b) a full-time student at the institution; or

    (c) an elected member of any local authority,

is not eligible for appointment as a member of the corporation otherwise than as a co-opted member.

(5) For the purposes of this paragraph, a person who is not for the time being enrolled as a student at the institution shall be treated as such a student during any period when he has been granted leave of absence from the institution for the purposes of study or travel or for carrying out the duties of any office held by him in the student union at the institution.

(6) It shall be for the appointing authority to determine any question as to whether any person is qualified in accordance with the preceding provisions of this paragraph for appointment as a member of the corporation of any description or category.

*Numbers*

4.—(1) The corporation shall make a determination with respect to their membership numbers.

(2) Such a determination shall fix the number of members of each variable category of which the corporation are to consist, subject to the limits applicable in relation to that category in accordance with paragraph 3 above.

(3) In making such a determination, the corporation shall secure that at least half of all the members of the corporation, when constituted in accordance with the determination, will be independent members.

(4) Such a determination shall not have effect so as to terminate the appointment of any person who is a member of the corporation at the time when it takes effect.

(5) Such a determination may be varied by a subsequent determination.

*Appointments*

5.—(1) Subject to section 124C of this Act, no appointment of members of the corporation may be made before the first determination of the corporation in accordance with paragraph 4 above takes effect.

(2) Subject to that section, the corporation are the appointing authority in relation to the appointment of any member of the corporation other than an independent member.

(3) Where an appointment of an additional independent member of the corporation falls to be made in consequence of a determination in accordance with paragraph 4 above, the appointing authority in relation to the appointment—

    (a) shall be the corporation if the appointment is made within the period of three months beginning with the date of the determination; or

    (b) if the appointment is not made within that period, shall be the current independent members of the corporation.

(4) Where a vacancy in the office of an independent member of the corporation arises on any existing independent member ceasing to hold office on the expiry of his term of office—

    (a) his successor shall not be appointed more than six months before the expiry of that term; and

    (b) the appointing authority in relation to the appointment of his successor—

        (i) shall be the corporation if the appointment is made not less than three months before the expiry of that term; or

        (ii) if the appointment is not so made, shall be the current independent members of the corporation.

(5) Where a vacancy in the office of an independent member of the corporation arises on the death of any such member or on any such member ceasing to hold office in accordance with the instrument, the appointing authority in relation to the appointment of his successor—

> (a) shall be the corporation if the appointment is made within the period of three months beginning with the date of death or the the date on which the office becomes vacant (as the case may be); or

> (b) if the appointment is not made within that period, shall be the current independent members of the corporation.

(6) No appointment of an independent member of the corporation by the corporation in accordance with sub-paragraph (3)(a), (4)(b)(i) or (5)(a) above shall be made unless the appointment has been approved by the current independent members of the corporation.

(7) If the number of independent members of the corporation falls below the number needed in accordance with its articles of government for a quorum, the Secretary of State is the appointing authority in relation to the appointment of such number of independent members as is required for a quorum.

### *Tenure of office etc.*

6. Subject to any other requirements of this Act, the instrument may provide for the eligibility of persons for membership of the corporation and shall provide for their period of office and the circumstances in which they are to cease to hold office.

### *Officers*

7. The instrument shall provide for one or more officers to be chosen from among the members.

### *Committees*

8. The instrument may provide for the corporation to establish committees and permit such committees to include persons who are not members of the corporation.

### *Allowances*

9. The instrument may provide for the corporation to pay allowances to its members.

### *Seal of corporation*

10. The instrument shall provide for the authentication of the application of the seal of the corporation.

### *Interpretation*

11. References in this Schedule, in relation to a corporation, to a variable category of members are references to any category of members in relation to which the number applicable in accordance with paragraph 3 above is subject to variation."

# SCHEDULE 7

## TRANSFERS: SUPPLEMENTARY PROVISIONS

### *Proof of title by certificate*

1. The Education Assets Board may issue a certificate stating that any property specified in the certificate, or any such interest in or right over any such property as may be so specified, or any right or liability so specified, was or was not transferred by virtue of this Act to any body corporate or persons so specified; and any such certificate shall be conclusive evidence for all purposes of that fact.

### *Construction of agreements*

2.—(1) Where any rights or liabilities transferred by virtue of this Act are rights or liabilities under an agreement to which the transferor was a party immediately before the date on which the transfer took effect (referred to in this Schedule as the "transfer date"), the agreement shall, unless the context otherwise requires, have effect on and after the transfer date as if—

   (a) the transferee had been a party to the agreement,

   (b) for any reference (whether express or implied and, if express, however worded) to the transferor there were substituted, as respects anything falling to be done on or after the transfer date, a reference to the transferee,

   (c) any reference (whether express or implied and, if express, however worded) to a specified officer of the transferor or a person employed by the transferor in a specified capacity were, as respects anything falling to be done on or after the transfer date, a reference to such person as the transferee may appoint or, in default of appointment, to an officer or employee of the transferee who corresponds as closely as possible to the person referred to in the agreement,

   (d) where the agreement refers to property, rights or liabilities which fall to be apportioned or divided between the transferor and the transferee, the agreement constituted two separate agreements separately enforceable by and against the transferor and the transferee as regards the part of the property, rights or liabilities retained by the transferor or (as the case may be) the part vesting in the transferee, and not as regards the other part,

and paragraph (d) above shall apply in particular to the covenants, stipulations and conditions of any lease by or to the transferor.

(2) This paragraph applies to any agreement whether in writing or not and whether or not of such a nature that rights and liabilities under it could be assigned by the transferor.

3.—(1) Without prejudice to the generality of paragraph 2 above, the transferee under a transfer made by virtue of this Act and any other person shall, as from the transfer date, have the same rights, powers and remedies (and in particular the same rights and powers as to the taking or resisting of legal proceedings or the making or resisting of applications to any authority) for ascertaining, perfecting or enforcing any right or liability transferred to and vested in the transferee by virtue of this Act as he would have had if that right or liability had at all times been a right or liability of the transferee.

(2) Any legal proceedings or applications to any authority pending on the transfer date by or against the transferor, in so far as they relate to any property, right or liability transferred to the transferee by virtue of this Act, or to any agreement relating to any such property, right or liability, shall be continued by or against the transferee to the exclusion of the transferor.

4. The provisions of paragraphs 2 and 3 above shall have effect for the interpretation of agreements subject to the context, and shall not apply where the context otherwise requires.

## SCHEDULE 8

### MINOR AND CONSEQUENTIAL AMENDMENTS

#### PART I

##### AMENDMENTS OF THE EDUCATION ACTS

*The Education Act 1944 (c. 31)*

1. The Education Act 1944 is amended as follows.

2. The duty imposed on local education authorities by section 7 (stages and purposes of statutory system of education) does not extend to matters in respect of which the higher education funding councils or the further education funding councils have a duty.

3. Section 8(3) is omitted.

4. In section 9(1) for "duties" there is substituted "functions".

5. In section 55 (provision of transport and other facilities)—

(a) for subsection (1) there is substituted—

"(1) A local education authority shall make such arrangements for the provision of transport and otherwise as they consider necessary or as the Secretary of State may direct for the purpose of facilitating the attendance of persons receiving education—

    (a) at schools,

    (b) at any institution maintained or assisted by them which provides higher education or further education (or both),

    (c) at any institution within the further education sector, or

    (d) at any institution outside the further education sector and higher education sector, where a further education funding council has secured provision for those persons at the institution under section 4(3) or (5) of the Further and Higher Education Act 1992;

and any transport provided in pursuance of such arrangements shall be provided free of charge."

(b) in subsection (2) for "pupil in attendance" there is substituted "person receiving education",

(c) in subsection (3) for "pupil", in each place, there is substituted "person",

(d) for subsection (4) there is substituted—

"(4) Arrangements made by a local education authority under subsection (1) above shall make provision—

    (a) for pupils at grant-maintained schools which is no less favourable than the provision made in pursuance of the arrangements for pupils at schools maintained by a local education authority,

SCH. 8

    (b) for persons receiving full-time education at any institution within the further education sector which is no less favourable than the provision made in pursuance of the arrangements for pupils of the same age at schools maintained by a local education authority, and

    (c) for persons receiving full-time education at institutions mentioned in subsection (1)(d) above which is no less favourable than the provision made in pursuance of the arrangements—

        (i) for persons of the same age with learning difficulties (within the meaning of section 41(9) of this Act) at schools maintained by a local education authority, or

        (ii) where there are no such arrangements, for such persons for whom the authority secures the provision of education at any other institution.", and

  (e) after subsection (4) there is added—

1980 c. 20.

"(5) Regulations under section 8(5) of the Education Act 1980 may require publication, within the meaning of that section, by every local education authority of such information as may be required by the regulations with respect to the authority's policy and arrangements for provision under this section for persons attending institutions mentioned in subsection (1)(c) or (d) above who are over compulsory school age and who have not attained the age of nineteen years."

6. At the end of section 56 (power to provide primary and secondary education otherwise than at school) (which becomes subsection (1)) there is added—

"(2) In this section "secondary education" includes any full-time education suitable to the requirements of persons over compulsory school age who have not attained the age of nineteen years and, for the purposes of the Education Acts 1944 to 1992—

  (a) any such education, or education similar in other respects but less than full-time, provided in pursuance of this section is to be treated as secondary education; and

  (b) any person for whom education is provided in pursuance of this section is to be treated as a pupil."

7. In section 62(1) (duties of Secretary of State and of local education authorities as to the training of teachers), after "grant-maintained schools" there is inserted "institutions within the further education sector".

8. Section 67(4A) (determination of disputes and questions - part-time senior education and post-school age education) is omitted.

9. Section 68 (power of Secretary of State to prevent unreasonable exercise of functions) shall apply in relation to a further education funding council or the governing body of an institution within the further education sector as it applies in relation to a local education authority or, as the case may be, the governors of a county or voluntary school.

10. Section 77 (inspection of educational establishments) shall cease to have effect in relation to any institution other than a school.

11. In section 81 (power of local education authorities to give assistance by means of scholarships and otherwise)—

  (a) for "pupils" (where it first appears) there is substituted "persons", and

  (b) in paragraph (c)—

       (i) for "pupils" (where it first appears) there is substituted "persons", and

       (ii) the words from "including" to the end are omitted.

12. In section 85(2) and (3) (power of local education authorities to accept gifts for educational purposes), the words "for providing primary or secondary education" are omitted.

13.—(1) Section 114 (interpretation) is amended as follows.

(2) In subsection (1)—

   (a) in the definition of "further education", after "section forty-one of this Act" there is added "as read with section 14 of the Further and Higher Education Act 1992",

   (b) the definitions of "part-time senior education" and "post-school age education" are omitted,

   (c) for the definition of "primary school" there is substituted—

      ""Primary school" means, subject to regulations under section 1 of the Education Act 1964, a school for providing primary education, whether or not it also provides further education", 1964 c. 82.

   (d) for the definition of "pupil" there is substituted—

      ""Pupil" has the meaning assigned to it by section 14(6) of the Further and Higher Education Act 1992",

   (e) for the definition of "school" there is substituted—

      ""School" has the meaning assigned to it by section 14(5) of the Further and Higher Education Act 1992",

   (f) in the definition of "secondary education", for "eight of this Act" there is substituted "14 of the Further and Higher Education Act 1992", and

   (g) for the definition of "secondary school" there is substituted—

      ""Secondary school" means, subject to regulations under section 1 of the Education Act 1964, a school for providing secondary education, whether or not it also provides primary or further education".

(3) Subsections (1A), (1B) and (1C) are omitted.

(4) In subsection (2A)—

   (a) for "PCFC funding sector" there is substituted "higher education sector other than a university", and

   (b) after "any institution" there is inserted "within the further education sector or".

### *The Education Act 1946 (c. 50)*

14. In the First Schedule to the Education Act 1946 (maintenance of voluntary schools) after paragraph 8 there is added—

   "9. Paragraph 8 of this Schedule shall not apply in the case of an institution which is or has at any time been within the further education sector."

### *The Education (Miscellaneous Provisions) Act 1948 (c. 40)*

15. Section 3(3) of the Education (Miscellaneous Provisions) Act 1948 (allocation between primary and secondary education of children between ten and a half and twelve years old - definition of secondary education) is omitted.

SCH. 8      16. In section 5(3) of that Act (amendment and consolidation of enactments as to provision of clothing) after paragraph (a) there is inserted—

"(aa)  for persons who have not attained the age of nineteen years and who are receiving education at an institution within the further education sector".

### The Education Act 1980 (c. 20)

17. After section 22(3A) of the Education Act 1980 (school meals - England and Wales) there is inserted—

"(3B) Subsection (1) above applies in relation to persons, other than pupils, who receive education at a school maintained by a local education authority or a grant-maintained school, and in relation to the authority maintaining the school or the governing body of the grant-maintained school, as it applies in relation to pupils at a school maintained by a local education authority and the authority maintaining the school; and an authority or governing body must charge for anything so provided and must charge every such person the same price for the same quantity of the same item."

### The Education Act 1981 (c. 60)

18. In section 14(2) of the Education Act 1981 (discontinuance of maintained special schools - notice) after paragraph (a) there is inserted—

"(aa)  the appropriate further education funding council".

### The Education (Fees and Awards) Act 1983 (c. 40)

19. In section 1(3) of the Education (Fees and Awards) Act 1983 (fees at universities and further education establishments)—

(a)  for paragraph (b) there is substituted—

"(b)  any institution within the higher education sector", and

(b)  after paragraph (c) there is inserted—

"(ca)  any institution within the further education sector".

### The Further Education Act 1985 (c. 47)

20. At the end of section 1 of the Further Education Act 1985 (supply of goods and services through further education establishments) there is added—

"(4)  In this Act "institution" does not include a school."

21.—(1) In section 2(2) of that Act (power of LEAs to lend money for those purposes) for paragraphs (a) to (d) there is substituted—

"(a)  to a higher education corporation or further education corporation (within the meaning of the Further and Higher Education Act 1992);

(b)  in the case of the following institutions—

(i) an institution within the higher education sector which is not conducted by a higher education corporation;

(ii) an institution within the further education sector which is not conducted by a further education corporation; or

(iii) an institution which provides higher education or further education and is assisted by a local education authority,

to the governing body of the institution or, if it is conducted by a company, to the company; or

(c) to a body corporate in which such a corporation or company as is mentioned in paragraph (a) or (b) above has a holding such as is mentioned in subsection (8) below".

(2) In subsection (8) of that section for "(2)(d)" there is substituted "(2)(c)".

*The Education (No. 2) Act 1986 (c. 61)*

22. In section 43 of the Education (No. 2) Act 1986 (freedom of speech in universities, etc.)—

(a) in subsection (5)—

(i) for paragraph (aa) there is substituted-

"(aa) any institution other than a university within the higher education sector",

(ii) after paragraph (b) there is inserted—

"(ba) any institution within the further education sector", and

(iii) paragraph (c) is omitted, and

(b) in subsection (7) paragraph (b) and "or authorities maintaining or (as the case may be) assisting the establishment" are omitted.

23. In section 49(3) of that Act (appraisal of performance of teachers)—

(a) paragraphs (d) and (da) are omitted,

(b) after paragraph (da) there is inserted-

"(db) at any institution within the further education sector", and

(c) in paragraph (e) for "(da)" there is substituted "(db)".

24. In section 51 of that Act (recoupment)—

(a) in subsection (2)(b) the words from "made" to the end are omitted,

(b) subsections (5) and (6) are omitted,

(c) in subsection (8) for "(1) to (6)" there is substituted "(1) and (2)", and

(d) after subsection (12) there is added—

"(13) References in this section to a pupil, in relation to any school or other institution, include any person who receives education at the school or institution."

25. In section 52(1)(a) and (3) of that Act (recoupment : cross-border provisions) for "pupil", in each place, there is substituted "person".

26. In section 58 of that Act (travelling and subsistence allowances for governors of schools and establishments of further education)—

(a) subsections (3), (4) and (5)(a) are omitted, and

(b) in subsection (5)(ab) "and are not designated establishments of higher or further education" is omitted.

*The Education Reform Act 1988 (c. 40)*

27. The Education Reform Act 1988 is amended as follows.

28. In section 24(1)(b) (extension of certain provisions)—

(a) for the words from "a reference" to second "and" there is substituted "except in relation to a local education authority, a reference to",

(b) in sub-paragraph (ii) after "a university" there is inserted "or an institution within the higher education sector", and

SCH. 8                (c) after that sub-paragraph there is added—

"and

(iii) any institution within the further education sector".


29. In section 100 (provision of benefits and services for pupils by local education authorities), after subsection (1) there is inserted—

"(1A) Where—

(a) a local education authority are under a duty, or have power, to provide any benefits or services for persons, other than pupils, receiving education at a school; and

(b) the duty is to be performed, or the power may be exercised, both in relation to such persons at schools maintained by a local education authority and in relation to such persons at grant-maintained schools;

the authority shall in performing the duty, or in exercising the power, treat such persons at grant-maintained schools no less favourably (whether as to the benefits or services provided or as to the terms on which they are provided) than such persons at schools maintained by a local education authority."


30. In section 120 (functions of local education authorities with respect to higher and further education)—

(a) subsection (2) is omitted,

(b) in subsection (3)(b) for "living outside their area" there is substituted "from other areas",

(c) in subsection (4)—

(i) for "universities, institutions within the PCFC funding sector" there is substituted "institutions within the higher education sector", and

(ii) after "sector" there is inserted "or the further education sector", and

(d) subsections (6), (7), (8), (9)(a)(ii) and (9)(b) are omitted.


31. In section 122 (orders incorporating higher education institutions maintained by local education authorities) subsections (2) to (5) are omitted.


32. In section 123 (provisions supplementary to sections 121 and 122)—

(a) at the end of subsection (1) there is added "or which has become a higher education corporation by virtue of section 122A of this Act", and

(b) for subsection (3) there is substituted—

"(3) Schedule 7 to this Act has effect with respect to each higher education corporation established before the appointed day (within the meaning of section 124A of this Act) unless an instrument of government for the corporation made under that section has effect.

(4) A higher education corporation established under section 122 of this Act on or after that day for the purpose of conducting any institution shall be established initially under the name given in the order under that section establishing the corporation."

33. In section 124 (powers of a higher education corporation)—

(a) in subsection (2)(b) for "disabled students" there is substituted "students having learning difficulties within the meaning of section 41(9) of the Education Act 1944", and

(b) subsection (4) is omitted.

34. In section 128 (dissolution of higher education corporations)—

(a) in subsection (1)(b)—

(i) for sub-paragraphs (iii) and (iv) there is substituted—

"(iii) a higher education funding council", and

(ii) after those sub-paragraphs there is inserted—

"(v) a further education funding council",

(b) for subsection (4)(b) there is substituted—

"(b) the higher education funding council", and

(c) after subsection (5) there is added—

"(6) An order under this section may apply section 127 of this Act with such modifications as the Secretary of State may consider necessary or desirable."

35. Sections 131, 132 and 134 (Universities Funding Council and Polytechnics and Colleges Funding Council) are omitted.

36. In section 135 (inspection of accounts)—

(a) for subsection (1)(c) there is substituted—

"(c) any designated institution within the meaning of section 129A of this Act", and

(b) in subsection (2) for the words from "grants" to the end there is substituted "financial support has been given to them under section 65 of the Further and Higher Education Act 1992."

37. In section 136 (transfer to Polytechnics and Colleges Funding Council of property and staff of National Advisory Body for Public Sector Higher Education)—

(a) in subsection (2) for "Polytechnics and Colleges Funding Council" there is substituted "Higher Education Funding Council for England", and

(b) subsections (3) to (7) are omitted.

38. In section 137(2) (control of disposals of land) "or 129(3)" is omitted.

39. In section 157 (construction of instruments providing for institution ceasing to be maintained or assisted by local education authority)—

(a) in subsection (4)—

(i) the words "or assisted" in both places are omitted,

(ii) after "becomes" there is inserted "an institution within the further education sector", and

(iii) for "the PCFC funding sector" there is substituted "the higher education sector",

(b) subsection (5)(b) is omitted, and

(c) in subsection (6)—

      (i) at the beginning of paragraph (b) there is inserted "an institution within the further education sector or", and

      (ii) in that paragraph for "the PCFC funding sector" there is substituted "the higher education sector".

40. In section 158(2) (reports and returns) paragraphs (a)(i) and (iii) and (b) are omitted.

41. Section 159(2)(b) (information with respect to educational provision in institutions providing further or higher education - designated assisted institutions) is omitted.

42. In section 161 (interpretation of Part II) subsection (1)(c) is omitted.

43. In section 197 (Education Assets Board)—

  (a) in subsection (4) after "this Act" there is inserted "and section 36 of and Schedule 5 to the Further and Higher Education Act 1992",

  (b) in subsection (6) for "this Act" there is substituted "the Education Acts 1944 to 1992", and

  (c) after subsection (7) there is inserted—

"(7A) A local education authority shall give the Board, within such reasonable time as the Board may specify, such information as the Board may require for the purposes of the exercise of any of their functions under the Further and Higher Education Act 1992 or under section 126 or 130 of this Act.

(7B) The governing body of any institution within the further education sector or the higher education sector shall give the Board, within such reasonable time as the Board may specify, such information as the Board may require for the purpose of the exercise of any of their functions under the Education Acts 1944 to 1992."

44. In section 198(5) (transfers under Parts I and II) for "the Polytechnics and Colleges Funding Council" there is substituted "the higher education funding council".

45. In section 205 (procedure for exercise of University Commissioners' powers)—

  (a) for subsection (2)(d) there is substituted—

    "(d) the higher education funding council", and

  (b) subsection (6) is omitted.

46. In section 210 (grants for the education of travellers and displaced persons), after "local education authorities" (in subsections (1) and (3)(d)) there is inserted "or institutions within the further education sector".

47. In section 211 (grants in respect of special provision for immigrants)—

  (a) after paragraph (b) there is inserted—

    "(ba) the governing body of an institution within the further education sector", and

  (b) paragraph (c) is omitted.

48. In section 214(2)(a) (unrecognised degrees) after "Royal Charter or" there is inserted "by or under".

49. In section 218 (school and further and higher education regulations)—

    (a) in subsection (1)(f) for "pupils" there is substituted "persons receiving education",

    (b) in subsection (7)(b) for "pupils attending" there is substituted "persons receiving education at",

    (c) in subsection (10)—

        (i) after paragraph (a) there is inserted-

      "(aa) it is within the further education sector", and

        (ii) paragraph (b) is omitted, and

    (d) in subsection (11) for "the PCFC funding sector" there is substituted "the higher education sector in receipt of financial support under section 65 of the Further and Higher Education Act 1992".

50. In section 219 (powers of Secretary of State in relation to certain educational institutions) subsections (1)(b), (2)(d) and (e) and (3)(c)(ii) are omitted.

51.—(1) Section 220 (extension of functions of Audit Commission) is amended as follows.

  (2) In subsection (1)—

    (a) for "the Polytechnics and Colleges Funding Council, a higher education corporation" there is substituted—

      "(a) a higher education funding council or the governing body of an institution within the higher education sector",

    (b) for "the governing body" there is substituted—

      "(b) a further education funding council or the governing body of an institution within the further education sector, or

      (c) the governing body".

  (3) In subsection (2)—

    (a) for paragraphs (a) and (b) there is substituted—

      "(a) with respect to studies relating to a higher education funding council, the council;

      (b) with respect to studies relating to the governing body of an institution within the higher education sector, the higher education funding council or the governing body", and

    (b) after those paragraphs there is inserted—

      "(ba) with respect to studies relating to a further education funding council, the council;

      (bb) with respect to studies relating to the governing body of an institution within the further education sector, the appropriate further education funding council or the governing body".

  (4) For subsection (3) there is substituted—

    "(3) The Commission may, at the request of a higher education funding council or a further education funding council, give the council advice in connection with the discharge of the council's functions under section 124B(2)(b) or paragraph 18(2)(b) of Schedule 7 to this Act.

  (5) In subsection (4) after "a higher education corporation" there is inserted "a further education corporation".

52. In section 221 (avoidance of certain contractual terms) subsection (1)(c) and, in subsection (3), the definition of "relevant institution" are omitted.

53. In section 222 (application of employment law during financial delegation) subsection (2)(b) and, in subsection (3)(c), "or institutions required to be covered by schemes under section 139 of this Act" are omitted.

54. In section 227 (application to Wales) subsections (2) to (4) are omitted.

55. In section 230 (stamp duty)—

(a) in subsection (1) "section 136(2)" is omitted, and

(b) in subsection (3)—

(i) for paragraph (b) there is substituted—

"(b) an institution within the higher education sector",

(ii) paragraph (c)(ii) is omitted, and

(iii) after paragraph (c) there is inserted—

"(ca) an institution within the further education sector".

56. In section 232 (orders and regulations)—

(a) in subsection (2) "140(1), 141(6), 145(6), 151(4), 156(10)" is omitted,

(b) in subsection (3) "or 227" is omitted, and

(c) in subsection (4)(b) "227" is omitted.

57. In section 234 (meaning of "assisted" for the purposes of the 1944 Act and Acts construed as one with it)—

(a) in subsection (1) for "the PCFC funding sector" there is substituted "the higher education sector other than a university", and

(b) subsection (2)(b) is omitted.

58. In section 235 (general interpretation) subsection (2)(a) and (h) are omitted.

59. In Schedule 7 (Higher Education Corporations)—

(a) for paragraph 1(4) there is substituted—

"(4) A corporation may change their name with the consent of the Privy Council.",

(b) in paragraph 18—

(i) in sub-paragraph (2)(b) for "the Polytechnics and Colleges Funding Council" there is substituted "the higher education funding council", and

(ii) for sub-paragraph (5) there is substituted—

"(5) No person shall be qualified to be appointed auditor under that sub-paragraph except—

1989 c. 40.

(a) an individual, or firm, eligible for appointment as a company auditor under section 25 of the Companies Act 1989;

(b) a member of the Chartered Institute of Public Finance and Accountancy; or

(c) a firm each of the members of which is a member of that institute.", and

(c) paragraph 19 is omitted.

60. Schedule 8 (the funding councils and the assets board) shall cease to have effect so far as it relates to the Universities Funding Council and the Polytechnics and Colleges Funding Council.

61. Paragraphs 62 to 64 below shall have effect, in place of paragraph 3 of Schedule 10 (supplementary provisions with respect to transfers) in the case of any transfer by virtue of section 126 or 130 and in such a case references to that paragraph of Schedule 10 shall be construed as references to paragraphs 62 to 64 below.

62.—(1) The Education Assets Board may, in the case of any matter on which agreement is required to be reached under paragraph 2(1) of that Schedule—

(a) if it appears to them that it is unlikely that such an agreement will be reached, or

(b) if such an agreement has not been reached within such period as may be prescribed by regulations,

give a direction determining that matter, and may include in the direction any provision which might have been included in an agreement under that paragraph.

(2) A direction under sub-paragraph (1) above may be given before or after the transfer date.

(3) Any property, rights or liabilities required by a direction under this paragraph to be transferred to the transferee shall be regarded as having been transferred to, and by virtue of this Act vested in, the transferee accordingly.

(4) The Board shall, before giving a direction under this paragraph, give the transferor and the transferee such opportunity as may be prescribed by regulations to make representations.

63.—(1) The transferor or transferee, if dissatisfied with a determination under paragraph 62 above, may appeal to the Secretary of State.

(2) An appeal under this paragraph shall be made in accordance with regulations.

(3) The Secretary of State shall, before determining an appeal under this paragraph, give the appellant and the respondent such opportunity as may be prescribed by regulations to make representations.

(4) On an appeal under this paragraph the Secretary of State may—

(a) allow or dismiss the appeal or vary the determination of the Board, and

(b) give a direction accordingly under paragraph 62 above.

64.—(1) Regulations may prescribe the procedure to be followed in making any determination under paragraphs 62 and 63 above.

(2) The regulations may in particular—

(a) provide for a time limit within which representations and any supporting documents must be submitted,

(b) empower the determining authority to proceed to a determination taking into account only such written representations and supporting documents as were submitted within the time limit, and

(c) empower the determining authority to proceed to a determination, after giving the transferor and the transferee or, as the case may be, the appellant and the respondent written notice of their intention to do so, notwithstanding that no written representations were made within the time limit, if it appears to the determining authority that they have sufficient material before them to enable them to make a determination.

(3) In sub-paragraph (2) above the "determining authority" means the Board or the Secretary of State, as the case may be.

SCH. 8          (4) In this paragraph and paragraphs 62 and 63 above "regulations" means regulations made by the Secretary of State.

65. In paragraph 4 of that Schedule at the beginning there is inserted—

"(1) Where a transfer by virtue of section 126 or 130 relates to registered land, it shall be the duty of the transferor to execute any such instrument under the Land Registration Acts 1925 to 1986, to deliver any such certificate under those Acts and to do such other things under those Acts as he would be required to execute, deliver or do in the case of a transfer by agreement between the transferor and the transferee.

(2)".

66. In Schedule 12 (minor and consequential amendments) paragraphs 68, 69(2), 70, 100(2) and 101(4) are omitted.

### *The Education (Student Loans) Act 1990 (c. 6)*

67. In section 1(3)(a) of the Education (Student Loans) Act 1990 (loans for students)—

1988 c. 40.

(a) for "131 or 132 of the Education Reform Act 1988" there is substituted " 65 of the Further and Higher Education Act 1992", and

(b) for the words from "institutions designated" to "local education authorities" there is substituted "institutions receiving recurrent grants towards their costs from a further education funding council".

## PART II

### AMENDMENTS OF OTHER ACTS

### *The Public Records Act 1958 (c. 51)*

68. In Schedule 1 to the Public Records Act 1958 (definition of public records), in Part II of the Table at the end of paragraph 3 (organisations whose records are public records) there is inserted in the appropriate place—

"Further Education Funding Council for England.

Further Education Funding Council for Wales.

Higher Education Funding Council for England.

Higher Education Funding Council for Wales."

### *The Charities Act 1960 (c. 58)*

69.—(1) A further education corporation shall be an exempt charity for the purposes of the Charities Act 1960.

(2) Paragraph (e) of Schedule 2 to that Act (institutions connected with institutions which are exempt charities for the purposes of that Act by virtue of the preceding provisions of that Schedule) shall apply in relation to an institution conducted by a further education corporation as it applies in relation to an institution included in that Schedule above that paragraph.

### *The Veterinary Surgeons Act 1966 (c. 36)*

70. In Schedule 3 to the Veterinary Surgeons Act 1966 (exemptions from restrictions on practice of veterinary surgery), in the definition of "recognised institution" after paragraph (a)(i) there is inserted—

"(iA) an institution within the further education sector within the meaning of section 91(3) of the Further and Higher Education Act 1992".

*The Local Authorities (Goods and Services) Act 1970 (c. 39)*

71.—(1) Subject to sub-paragraph (2) below, in the Local Authorities (Goods and Services) Act 1970 (supply of goods and services by local authorities to public bodies) "public body" shall include any institution within the further education sector or the higher education sector.

(2) The provisions of sub-paragraph (1) above shall have effect as if made by an order under section 1(5) of that Act (power to provide that a person or description of persons shall be a public body for the purposes of that Act).

(3) An order under that section may accordingly vary or revoke the provisions of sub-paragraph (1) above as they apply to an institution within the further education sector or the higher education sector specified in the order.

*The Chronically Sick and Disabled Persons Act 1970 (c. 44)*

72. In section 8(2) of the Chronically Sick and Disabled Persons Act 1970 (access to, and facilities at, university and school buildings)—

  (a) for paragraph (aa) there is substituted—

      "(aa) institutions within the higher education sector within the meaning of section 91(5) of the Further and Higher Education Act 1992", and

  (b) after paragraph (b) there is inserted—

      "(ba) institutions within the further education sector within the meaning of section 91(3) of the Further and Higher Education Act 1992".

*The Superannuation Act 1972 (c. 11)*

73. In Schedule 1 to the Superannuation Act 1972 the entries relating to the Universities Funding Council and the Polytechnics and Colleges Funding Council are omitted.

*The House of Commons Disqualification Act 1975 (c. 24)*

74. In Part III of Schedule 1 to the House of Commons Disqualification Act 1975 the entries relating to the Polytechnics and Colleges Funding Council and the Universities Funding Council are omitted.

*The Sex Discrimination Act 1975 (c. 65)*

75. The Sex Discrimination Act 1975 is amended as follows.

76.—(1) The Table in section 22 (discrimination by bodies in charge of educational establishments) is amended as follows.

(2) After paragraph 3A there is inserted—

| | |
|---|---|
| "3B. Institution within the further education sector (within the meaning of section 91(3) of the Further and Higher Education Act 1992). | Governing body." |

(3) For paragraph 4A there is substituted—

| "4A. Institution, other than a university, within the higher education sector (within the meaning of section 91(5) of the Further and Higher Education Act 1992). | Governing body." |

(4) In paragraph 5 for "to 4" there is substituted "to 4A".

77. After that section there is inserted—

"Meaning of pupil in section 22.     22A. For the purposes of section 22, "pupil" includes, in England and Wales, any person who receives education at a school or institution to which that section applies."

78. After section 23 (other discrimination by local education authorities) there is inserted—

"Discrimination by Further Education and Higher Education Funding Councils     23A. It is unlawful for the Further Education Funding Council for England, the Further Education Funding Council for Wales, the Higher Education Funding Council for England or the Higher Education Funding Council for Wales in carrying out their functions under the Education Acts 1944 to 1992, to do any act which constitutes sex discrimination."

79.—(1) In section 25(6) (general duty in public sector of education)—

(a) in paragraph (c)(i), for "4A" there is substituted "3B", and

(b) after paragraph (c) there is added—

"(d) the Further Education Funding Council for England and the Further Education Funding Council for Wales."

(2) In relation to a further education corporation or a Further Education Funding Council the reference in section 25(2) to section 99 of the Education Act 1944 is to be read as a reference to section 57(3) of the Further and Higher Education Act 1992.

80. After section 26(3) (exception for single-sex establishments) there is added—

"(4) In this section, as it applies to an establishment in England and Wales, "pupil" includes any person who receives education at that establishment."

81. After section 27(5) (exception for single-sex establishments turning co-educational) there is added—

"(6) In this section, as it applies to an establishment in England and Wales, "pupil" includes any person who receives education at that establishment."

82. In section 82(1) (general interpretation provisions) in the definition of "further education", for "section 41(2)(a) of the Education Act 1944" there is substituted "section 41(3) of the Education Act 1944 as read with section 14 of the Further and Higher Education Act 1992".

83. For paragraph 4 of Schedule 2 (transitional exemption orders for educational admissions) there is substituted—

"4. Regulations under section 218 of the Education Reform Act 1988 may provide for the submission to the Secretary of State of an application for the making by him of a transitional exemption order in relation to any school or institution to which that section, or any part of that section, applies and which does not fall within paragraph 3 above, and for the making by him of the order."

Sch. 8
1988 c. 40.

*The Race Relations Act 1976 (c. 74)*

84. The Race Relations Act 1976 is amended as follows.

85.—(1) The Table in section 17 (discrimination by bodies in charge of educational establishments) is amended as follows.

(2) After paragraph 3A there is inserted—

| | |
|---|---|
| "3B. Institution within the further education sector (within the meaning of section 91(3) of the Further and Higher Education Act 1992). | Governing body." |

(3) For paragraph 4A there is substituted—

| | |
|---|---|
| "4A. Institution, other than a university, within the higher education sector (within the meaning of section 91(5) of the Further and Higher Education Act 1992). | Governing body." |

(4) In paragraph 5 for "to 4" there is substituted "to 4A".

86. After that section there is inserted—

"Meaning of pupil in section 17. 17A. For the purposes of section 17, "pupil" includes, in England and Wales, any person who receives education at a school or institution to which that section applies."

87. After section 18 (other discrimination by local education authorities) there is inserted—

"Discrimination by Further Education and Higher Education Funding Councils 18A. It is unlawful for the Further Education Funding Council for England, the Further Education Funding Council for Wales, the Higher Education Funding Council for England or the Higher Education Funding Council for Wales in carrying out their functions under the Education Acts 1944 to 1992, to do any act which constitutes racial discrimination."

88.—(1) In section 19(6) (general duty in public sector of education)—

(a) in paragraph (c)(i), for "4A" there is substituted "3B", and

(b) after paragraph (c) there is added—

"(d) the Further Education Funding Council for England and the Further Education Funding Council for Wales."

(2) In relation to a further education corporation or a Further Education Funding Council the reference in section 19(2) to section 99 of the Education Act 1944 is to be read as a reference to section 57(3) of the Further and Higher Education Act 1992.

1944 c. 31.

*The Employment Protection (Consolidation) Act 1978 (c. 44)*

89. In section 29(1) of the Employment Protection (Consolidation) Act 1978 (persons holding certain offices to be allowed time off for public duties), in paragraph (ef) after "governing body of a" there is inserted "further education corporation or".

*The Public Passenger Vehicles Act 1981 (c. 14)*

90. In section 46(3) of the Public Passenger Vehicles Act 1981 (fare-paying passengers on school buses) in the definition of "free school transport" for "pupils" there is substituted "persons".

*The Disabled Persons (Services, Consultation and Representation) Act 1986 (c. 33)*

91.—(1) Section 5 of the Disabled Persons (Services, Consultation and Representation) Act 1986 (disabled persons leaving special education) is amended as follows.

(2) for subsections (3) and (4) there is substituted—

"(3) In the following provisions of this section and in section 6 a person in respect of whom the appropriate officer has given his opinion that he is a disabled person is referred to as a "disabled student".

(3A) The responsible authority shall give to the appropriate officer written notification for the purposes of subsection (5) of the date on which any disabled student will cease to be of compulsory school age, and the notification shall state—

(a) his name and address; and

(b) whether or not he intends to remain in full-time education and, if he does, the name of the school or other institution at which the education will be received;

and shall be given not earlier than twelve months, nor later than eight months, before that date.

(3B) Where, in the case of a disabled student over compulsory school age who is receiving relevant full-time education, that is—

(a) full-time education at a school; or

(b) full-time further or higher education at an institution other than a school;

it appears to the responsible authority that the student will cease to receive relevant full-time education on a date ("the leaving date") on which he will be under the age of nineteen years and eight months, the responsible authority shall give written notification for the purposes of subsection (5) to the appropriate officer.

(3C) That notification shall state—

(a) his name and address; and

(b) the leaving date;

and shall be given not earlier than twelve months, nor later than eight months, before the leaving date.

(4) If at any time it appears to the responsible authority—

(a) that a disabled student has ceased to receive relevant full-time education or will cease to do so on a date less than 8 months after that time, and

(b) that no notification has been given under subsection (3B), but

(c) that, had the responsible authority for the time being been aware of his intentions 8 months or more before that date, they would have been required to give notification under that subsection with respect to him,

that authority shall, as soon as is reasonably practicable, give written notification for the purposes of subsection (5) to the appropriate officer of his name and address and of the date on which he ceased to receive, or will cease to receive, that education."

(3) In subsection (5)—

(a) for "any person under subsection (3)" there is substituted "a student under subsection (3A) that he does not intend to remain in full-time education or under subsection (3B)", and

(b) for "notification under subsection (3)" there is substituted "notification under subsection (3A) or (3B)".

(4) In subsection (6)—

(a) for "(3)" in both places there is substituted "(3A) that he does not intend to remain in full-time education or under subsection (3B)", and

(b) for the words from "a local education authority" to "establishment of further or higher education" there is substituted "the responsible authority that the person will be receiving relevant full-time education".

(5) In subsection (9) (interpretation)—

(a) in the definition of "child" after "school or" there is inserted "as a student at",

(b) in the definition of "the responsible authority" for paragraph (b) there is substituted—

"(b) in relation to a person receiving full-time further education or higher education at an institution within the further education sector or the higher education sector, means the governing body of the institution; and

(c) in relation to a person for whom a further education funding council has secured full-time further education at an institution (other than a school) outside the further education sector or the higher education sector, the council",

(c) after "the Education Act 1944" there is inserted "or the Further and Higher Education Act 1992", and

(d) for "that Act" there is substituted "those Acts".

92. For section 6(1) of that Act (review of expected leaving dates from full-time education of disabled persons) there is substituted—

"6.—(1) The responsible authority shall for the purposes of section 5 above keep under review the date when any disabled student is expected to cease to receive relevant full-time education."

*The Employment Act 1989 (c. 38)*

93. In section 5(6) of the Employment Act 1989 (exemption for discrimination in connection with certain educational appointments)—

(a) after paragraph (b) there is inserted—

"(ba) any institution designated by order under section 28 of the Further and Higher Education Act 1992", and

(b) for paragraph (c) there is substituted—

"(c) any institution designated by order made or having effect as if made under section 129 of the Education Reform Act 1988."

*The Town and Country Planning Act 1990 (c. 8)*

94. In section 76(1) of the Town and Country Planning Act 1990 (duty to draw attention to certain provisions for benefit of disabled)—

    (a) in paragraph (d) for "the PCFC funding sector" there is substituted "the higher education sector within the meaning of section 91(5) of the Further and Higher Education Act 1992", and

    (b) after paragraph (e) there is inserted—

        "(f) of a building intended for the purposes of an institution within the further education sector within the meaning of section 91(3) of the Further and Higher Education Act 1992".

*The Environmental Protection Act 1990 (c. 43)*

95. In section 98(2) of the Environmental Protection Act 1990 (definitions)—

    (a) paragraph (a) is omitted,

    (b) for paragraph (d) there is substituted—

        "(d) any institution within the higher education sector within the meaning of section 91(5) of the Further and Higher Education Act 1992", and

    (c) after paragraph (d) there is inserted—

        "(da) any institution within the further education sector within the meaning of section 91(3) of the Further and Higher Education Act 1992".

## SCHEDULE 9

### REPEALS

| Chapter | Short title | Extent of repeal |
|---|---|---|
| 1944 c. 31. | The Education Act 1944. | Section 8(3).<br>Section 67(4A).<br>In section 85(2) and (3) "for providing primary or secondary education".<br>In section 114(1), the definitions of "part-time senior education" and "post-school age education".<br>Section 114(1A), (1B) and (1C). |
| 1948 c. 40. | The Education (Miscellaneous Provisions) Act 1948. | Section 3(3). |
| 1972 c. 11. | The Superannuation Act 1972. | In Schedule 1 the entries relating to the Universities Funding Council and the Polytechnics and Colleges Funding Council. |

SCH. 9

| Chapter | Short title | Extent of repeal |
|---|---|---|
| 1975 c. 24. | The House of Commons Disqualification Act 1975. | In Part III of Schedule 1 the entries relating to the Polytechnics and Colleges Funding Council and the Universities Funding Council. |
| 1986 c. 61. | The Education (No. 2) Act 1986. | Section 43(5)(c) and, in subsection (7), paragraph (b) and "or authorities maintaining or (as the case may be) assisting the establishment".<br>Section 49(3)(d) and (da).<br>In section 51, in subsection (2)(b) the words from "made" to the end and subsections (5) and (6).<br>Section 58(3), (4) and (5)(a) and in subsection (5)(ab) "and are not designated establishments of higher or further education". |
| 1988 c. 40. | The Education Reform Act 1988. | In section 105(2)(b) "but not the age of nineteen years".<br>Section 120(2), (6), (7), (8), (9)(a)(ii) and (9)(b).<br>Section 122(2) to (5).<br>Section 124(4).<br>Section 129(3) and (4).<br>Sections 131 and 132.<br>Section 134.<br>Section 136(3) to (7).<br>In section 137(2) "or 129(3)".<br>Chapter III of Part II.<br>Section 156.<br>In section 157 the words "or assisted" in both places in subsection (4) and subsection (5)(b).<br>Section 158(2)(a)(i) and (iii) and (b).<br>Section 159(2)(b).<br>Section 161(1)(c).<br>Section 205(6).<br>Section 211(c).<br>Section 218(10)(b).<br>Section 219(1)(b), (2)(d) and (e) and (3)(c)(ii).<br>In section 221, subsection (1)(c) and, in subsection (3), the definition of "relevant institution".<br>In section 222, subsection (2)(b) and, in subsection (3)(c), "or institutions required to be covered by schemes under section 139 of this Act". |

| Chapter | Short title | Extent of repeal |
|---|---|---|
| | | Section 227(2) to (4). In section 230, in subsection (1) "section 136(2)" and subsection (3)(c)(ii). In section 232, in subsection (2) "140(1), 141(6), 145(6), 151(4), 156(10)", in subsection (3) "or 227" and in subsection (4)(b) "227". Section 234(2)(b). Section 235(2)(a) and (h). Paragraph 19 of Schedule 7. Paragraphs 68, 69(2), 70, 100(2) and 101(4) of Schedule 12. |
| 1990 c. 43. | The Environmental Protection Act 1990. | Section 98(2)(a). |

**PRINTED IN THE UNITED KINGDOM BY PAUL FREEMAN**
Controller and Chief Executive of Her Majesty's Stationery Office
and Queen's Printer of Acts of Parliament

HMSO publications are available from:

**HMSO Publications Centre**
(Mail, fax and telephone orders only)
PO Box 276, London SW8 5DT
Telephone orders 071-873 9090
General enquiries 071-873 0011
(queuing system in operation for both numbers)
Fax orders 071-873 8200

**HMSO Bookshops**
49 High Holborn, London WC1V 6HB   071-873 0011 (Counter service only)
258 Broad Street, Birmingham B1 2HE   021-643 3740
Southey House, 33 Wine Street, Bristol BS1 2BQ   (0272) 264306
9-21 Princess Street, Manchester M60 8AS   061-834 7201
80 Chichester Street, Belfast BT1 4JY   (0232) 238451
71 Lothian Road, Edinburgh EH3 9AZ   031-228 4181

**HMSO's Accredited Agents**
**(see Yellow Pages)**

*And through good booksellers*

ISBN 0-10-541392-5

9 780105 413929